The Talented Student

The Talented Student

A Validation of the Creativity-Intelligence Distinction

Michael A. Wallach and
Cliff W. Wing, Jr.
Duke University

Holt, Rinehart and Winston, Inc.
New York Chicago San Francisco Atlanta Dallas
Montreal Toronto London Sydney

Copyright © 1969 by Holt, Rinehart and Winston, Inc.
Library of Congress Catalog Card Number: 69-17663

03-079800-0

Printed in the United States of America

1 2 3 4 5 6 7 8 9

Preface

As we look around us in the world, we can find examples of excellence in the pursuit of diverse human activities. One person displays consummate skill as a writer of novels, another is an effective leader of men, someone else has pursued a scientific question to the point of obtaining fundamental insight into the structure of matter, still another is a sensitive performer of music, another is an artist whose graphic designs bring pleasure to the eye, and somebody else is an actor whose voice and gestures communicate the pathos of a tragic hero to an audience. These forms of talented functioning testify to what man is capable of at his best. Their exercise defines what a free society is about: nourishment and advancement of the full range of human potential among its members.

How shall this potential be nourished? Even in a wealthy society, there inevitably will be a scarcity of resources for preferential treatment relative to demand. Only a small proportion of the students who desire admission to prestigious graduate schools can be accepted; only a fraction of the students who apply for financial support can receive it. On what basis, then, does one select some as more deserving than others? Almost invariably, the answer to this question has been: in terms of scores on intelligence tests. Why in terms of intelligence level? Because, so the customary answer runs, intelligence tests indicate a student's potential for academic achievement. But at this point the reasoning becomes murky. Grades are not—or at least, ought not to be —an end in themselves. It is not grades that we are interested in maximizing; rather, it is ultimate real-life accomplishments. What do grades predict about life? As near as one can tell from available research, surprisingly little.

In this volume we report an investigation of talented accomplishments outside the classroom during the high school years and what they seem to imply about cognitive processes. Extracurricular attainments in the exercise of leadership, in various arts, in scientific endeavors, and in social services tell us something about what a student undertakes in that sector of his life where—unlike the case with academic achievement—he is, by and large, doing what he wants to do rather than what society requires of him. We suspected that self-initiated accomplishments would be more representative of a person's characteristic functioning under the real-life conditions he encounters when formal schooling is over than would academic grades. But be that as it may, we were investigating here actual examples of fulfilled talents as they manifest themselves in the lives of young people: attainments that are important and valuable in their own right and hence eminently worthy of support.

What we have found can be put quite directly. Within the intelligence range defined by our sample—and it is a sample that falls overall within the upper part of the intelligence continuum—intelligence level is indeed strongly related to grades. But only to grades. Intelligence is not at all related to level or quality of attainment in any of the diverse forms of extracurricular involvement that we studied—and these covered the entire range from literary and artistic pursuits through dramatic and musical performance, social service activities, and scientific work on one's own to leadership in student organizations. On the other hand, a person's resourcefulness in generating ideas—what may best be understood as his typical degree of energy with respect to producing thoughts—although it cannot be predicted from intelligence level, is substantially related to the quality of his contribution in all extracurricular domains that share a common emphasis upon innovation of one kind or another: namely, leadership, where political strategems and plans for political action are formed; art, where paintings, drawings, and sculpture are created; writing, where words are turned into poetry or prose; and scientific work, where plans for research are developed and carried out.

In a word, then, intelligence is indicative of academic grades, but it is irrelevant to the display of any of the forms of extracurricular accomplishments we investigated. Ideational resourcefulness—something very different from intelligence—is what proves to be important once we step outside the classroom. Information about who produces ideas helps identify the students who display talented nonacademic attainments in any of a diverse range of endeavors in which innovation plays a major role.

But who is more likely to be an important writer in his adult years—the student who publishes poetry and prose now, or the student who earns a higher grade point average? Who is more likely to become a scientific innovator—the student who demonstrates a penchant for scientific innovation through clever experimentation on his own, or the student who earns a higher grade point average? Of whom does it seem more reasonable to expect adult leadership as a statesman—the student who is elected president or chairman of a student organization, or the student who earns a higher grade point average? Who is more likely to contribute to the graphic arts as an adult—the student who tries his hand at it now, or the student who earns a higher grade point average? If we believe these queries should be answered in favor of the high academic achiever, then it makes sense to use intelligence level as a definition of talent. The evidence, however, does not point to a link between academic achievement and degree of contribution to society as an adult. We are left, then, with the strong suspicion that persistence forecasting offers the most accurate basis for prediction— that students who excel at self-initiated activities will go on to make meaningful contributions as adults. Assessment of intelligence level in our study did not identify these students, but assessment of the typical level of ideational productivity, or what we might call the degree of cognitive vitality, did identify them.

The implications of these findings for practices of preferential selection are not far to seek. Intelligence differences were not associated with meaningful talented accomplishments of any kind. Differences in ideational resourcefulness were. The burden of proof is decidedly on the champion of intelligence assessment, therefore, if he wishes to argue that it is useful to make intelligence discriminations among the members of our sample. One must travel routes other than that of intelligence testing in order to comprehend —and hence also to foster—the manifestations of talent. Such routes will be explored in what follows.

We address this book to readers of two kinds. As a primary report of previously unpublished research concerning the nature of talent it is addressed to colleagues and students in psychology and education. As an investigation with results that bear upon the question of how selection should proceed when discriminations must be made between young people deemed more or less worthy of the forms of support and advancement the society can provide, it is addressed to a second audience, namely, those who make and carry out student selection policy. In seeking to interest both audiences in what we have to say, we are putting into practice a belief which in fact has guided the development of our research enterprise as a whole: that substantive contributions concerning the psychology of talent and actual practices concerning the selection of talented students for preferential treatment of one sort or another need to be kept in close contact. If the empirical findings obtained by the "pure" researcher do in fact make for a clear advancement in our theoretical understanding, they ought to have an impact upon the selection operations that define talent in the society. We feel it appropriate to address both the researcher and the practitioner with the findings presented in this book.

Although our goal has been to speak as plainly as possible, the methodological and statistical details of the research nevertheless are presented in full for those readers who wish to examine them. The general reasoning behind our procedure can be followed without special technical knowledge, as can the interpretation of our results. We did not stop to explain such statistical tools, however, as the standard deviation, standard scores, the correlation coefficient, the t test, and χ^2. The reader who is unfamiliar with statistics will therefore be in the position of having to take our word for the meaning of certain aspects of the work. The context will indicate which material can be skimmed. The more technical-minded reader, on the other hand, will find descriptions of all the specifics he would want for a complete understanding of the operations and the analyses that were carried out.

For research assistance in conducting the present investigation, we are grateful to Lynn Clark, Jerry Downing, and Marilyn Petersen. Financial aid was provided in part by a grant from the Richardson Foundation and in part by Duke University. The data of the study were analyzed at the Duke University Computing Laboratory, which is supported in part by a grant from the National Science Foundation.

Thanks are due Holt, Rinehart and Winston, Inc., for permission to reproduce from Figures 2 and 3 of *Modes of Thinking in Young Children* (Wallach and Kogan, 1965) the stimulus materials that appear in Figure 1 of the present volume. Finally, we are grateful to Judy Edquist for her secretarial assistance.

MICHAEL A. WALLACH
CLIFF W. WING, JR.

Durham, North Carolina
April, 1968

Table of Contents

The Talented Student

Chapter 1

The Two Theses

What is intelligence? Typical definitions, such as that provided by Wechsler (1952), refer to the individual's ability to pursue rational problem-solving strategies in dealing with whatever environmental contingencies may arise. This ability usually is indexed according to a person's level of skill in working with verbal and numerical concepts in various situations requiring interpretation and reasoning — such concepts presumably constituting the major cognitive tools that can be brought to bear when a problem in the real world presents itself for solution. Something like the degree of articulateness of one's conceptual apparatus seems to be what is meant here: the elaborateness of one's informational storehouse and the ease with which relevant information can be retrieved or made available for use in response to situational demands.

There is no doubt that intelligence is of great importance as a basis for predicting a person's competence in school. The documentation linking intelligence with academic achievement has been extensive indeed (see, for example, Edwards and Tyler, 1965; Wallach and Kogan, 1965). From such documentation has arisen a very strong reliance upon the use of intelligence assessors in defining the worthiness of a person for receiving the rewards that society can bestow — such as selection for a scholarship or for higher education at a superior college. Such reliance certainly comes as no surprise. Furthermore, in its justification we can cite not only the power of intelligence tests to predict academic grades — that is, the validity of intelligence tests in terms of a criterion of classroom achievement — but also the culture's essentially egalitarian ideology regarding selection procedures. For intelligence, after all, presumably refers to an at least relatively culture-fair assessment of a person's talent — an assessment that at least to some degree cuts through the benefits that accrue from superior socio-economic background. Use of intelligence tests should, therefore, provide a relatively democratic basis for determining who shall have maximum access to the benefits and opportunities available in a social context where scarcity of resources necessitates some degree of selectivity.

The increased usage and methodological refinement of intelligence assessors in our society over the last twenty-five years or so have in fact achieved a considerable broadening of access to opportunities for advancement within the culture. No longer is attendance at selective colleges, for example, the prerogative of the privileged few for whom the accident of birth would render such attendance a foregone conclusion. Demonstrations of intellectual competence have tended to replace ascriptive criteria of social status and cultural background as grounds for admission — no mean accomplishment for a time span of two and one-half decades. The enthusiasm for intelligence assessment as a means of carrying out selection thus is well grounded, both in terms of the values of a democratic society and in terms of validation against the criterion of school achievement. This enthusiasm has carried

in its wake, however, what we believe to be a damaging mis-
conception regarding the value of intelligence tests.

The first thesis of this book is that, while intelligence
information is highly useful for predicting academic forms
of achievement, such information is useless when it comes
to predicting a range of talented accomplishments outside
the classroom that are of undeniable social worth. Because
intelligence has become such a salient dimension for evaluating human competence, its validity is assumed to extend
well beyond criteria of grade achievement in school. We
intend to demonstrate, however, that within a sample for
which there is an intelligence range sufficient to generate a
sizeable relationship between intelligence and the usual
criteria of academic achievement, no relationship will be
found between intelligence and various indicators of talented
accomplishments in spheres outside of one's grade point
average. Some would argue that these nonacademic or extracurricular forms of talented accomplishments come closer
to representing what accomplishment is like in the years
after formal schooling is over than is the case for academic
achievement. In this sense, talented accomplishments outside
the classroom would possess greater representativeness of
real-life functioning or what Brunswik (1956) would call
greater "ecological validity" than would the accumulation
of a high academic average in school. Thus, for instance,
Hoyt (1966), in an extensive review of the literature, found
college grades to possess surprisingly little relationship to
criteria of accomplishment in various occupations undertaken
after completion of schooling, no matter how such accomplishment was defined. Were this first thesis to be sustained,
therefore, we could question whether intelligence tests have
the range of predictive power that tends to be imputed to
them. We would have a basis for proposing that if one wishes
to comprehend who will exhibit the forms of talented nonacademic accomplishments in question, intelligence testing
will not provide the answer.

A further word is in order concerning the kind of population to whom we deem our thesis to be applicable. We are not talking about a group characterized by maximum heterogeneity with regard to intelligence, for at a sufficiently high degree of intelligence spread it is inevitable that intelligence will be somewhat associated with every good thing under the sun. Every kind of talented accomplishment, after all, requires some minimum quantum of ability to deal with concepts and to solve problems: the creative writer needs facility in dealing with the language, the artist must understand what effect will be produced by a given technique of painting, the inventor must be able to reason. Rather, we are talking about a population scoring chiefly in the upper reaches on the general intelligence continuum — in a word, the kind of population represented by college students in selective colleges. The issue that we address is how ability ought to be conceptualized in the case of students who already have been deemed competent enough to have earned acceptance to college. The crucial point for our first thesis is that the intelligence range under consideration — that represented by college students — still must be sufficiently broad that we can show intelligence differences to be substantially linked with academic achievement within our sample. Then, despite this relationship between intelligence and earning higher grades, we want to show that the same intelligence differences possess no relationship at all to various criteria of talented accomplishment in the world beyond the schoolhouse. It goes without saying, of course, that we must also be able to establish contrasts within our sample concerning greater and lesser degrees of the nonacademic types of talented accomplishments in question: we could make little headway if all of the students exhibited these attainments, or if none of them did. This is a point to which we shall return when we move on to consider our second thesis. In sum, then, meaningful demonstration of nonrelationship between intelligence differences and talented accomplish-

ments outside the classroom — our first thesis — requires
that we also show two things: first, that the intelligence
differences were great enough to replicate the well-known
strong relationship between intelligence and academic achievement indicators; and second, that there was a goodly amount
of variation in the assessments of nonacademic talented accomplishments. How much is a "goodly amount?" The best
answer would seem to be: enough to produce meaningful
relationships with something else. But that gets us ahead
of our story.

What do we mean, then, by nonacademic talented
accomplishments? Among the accomplishments that we
would classify as nonacademic — that is, not the type that
earns grade credits — are, for example, signs of leadership in
one's relations with one's fellows (as indicated by election to
the presidency of one's student government or appointment to
an administrative post in a student organization); signs of
talent in the visual arts (as exemplified by painting pictures
and displaying them in an exhibition or winning an award
in an art competition); signs of expertise in literary activities
(as testified by writing poetry for one's own pleasure, pub-
lishing original writings in a magazine, or winning a literary
prize for one's achievements in the area of creative writing);
signs of competence at extracurricular enterprises in the field
of science (as reflected in the construction of a piece of scientific apparatus for an experiment that one is conducting
on one's own, gaining an appointment as a laboratory assistant in a science course, or winning a prize for a science
project submitted for judgment at a state or regional science
contest); and signs of accomplishment in musical activities
(as indicated by playing a musical instrument, singing, or performing as a regular professional musician).

In order to make it possible for the individual to attain
accomplishments such as these, he must be old enough to
have had the time to amass the necessary forms of expertise,
we must be considering a time period extensive enough to

offer the possibility of an adequate range of opportunities having been presented for such activities, and it must furthermore be a time period sufficiently free from the pressure of strictly academic tasks that the individual would have had the leisure to engage in these nonacademic activities if so inclined. All three considerations obviously point to the four-year period of high school attendance as the relevant time zone to consider. The high school years constitute a period during which there is a relatively rare uniting of the leisure to pursue varied directions of interests with the possibility of having amassed sufficient technical competence to make the pursuit worthwhile. The full four years of high school, furthermore, represent a sufficiently long time sample that the student has had a good chance to explore and sense his potential and relative facility in various lines of nonacademic pursuits. We chose to explore matters of talented nonacademic attainments, therefore, with students who, as entering freshmen at college, were looking back upon their activities during the high school period. At college entrance time, the record of high school attainments would be both complete and most accurately remembered.

The impetus for studying nonacademic forms of talented accomplishments comes most directly from a recent series of pioneering studies by Holland, Richards, and their collaborators (see, for example, Holland, 1961, 1967; Holland and Nichols, 1964; Holland and Richards, 1965, 1966, 1967; and Richards, Holland, and Lutz, 1966, 1967). Their interest has been to show that academic and nonacademic forms of accomplishment are minimally related to each other, and this they have documented in various ways. With expression of nonacademic talents inferred from student reports concerning the types of signs that we mentioned before, these investigators found, for example, relatively low relationships between such talented accomplishments and academic achievement indicators not only in a very high-ability group of high school seniors — National Merit Scholarship Finalists — but also in broader samples of college students. We note that the use of retrospective reporting by the students about these matters does not seem to introduce any serious issues concerning veridicality because of the following considerations: at least in the case of the college student samples, no rational goal — such as college admission — could be viewed as dependent upon how one answered the questions; even when admission to college *is* at issue and one is asking about as relevant a matter as grades, data from Davidsen (1963) yielded a correlation of .92 between self-reported high school grades and the actual grade records themselves; meaningful patterns emerged among different domains of nonacademic accomplishment that could not be accounted for in terms of a sheer disposition to endorse or say yes to any kind of self-report item — that is, a response set to agree regardless of a question's content. It is clear nevertheless that in research of this kind one must make sure the students have been convinced that nothing of importance to them is contingent upon how they respond so there will be a minimal impetus to falsify, and one must check on the degree of emergence of psychologically meaningful differences in the relationships surrounding various self-report questions as a means of insuring against the operation of a blanket tendency to agree whatever the content. Both matters were of concern to us in the research that we shall describe.

We built quite directly upon the Holland-Richards line of work in terms of methods for assessing nonacademic forms of talented accomplishment, but from a somewhat different perspective. While their goal was the demonstration of minimal relationships between academic and nonacademic types of accomplishment, and we certainly know that academic forms of achievement ought to be strongly related to intelligence, our goal — as set forth in previous pages — was to demonstrate independence between direct assessors of general intelligence and nonacademic accomplishments of various sorts. Why did this further step seem necessary? Why could we not simply let the matter rest where the Holland-Richards research had left it — namely, at the point of demonstrating minimal relationships between academic achievement and nonacademic accomplishments? Because of some recent criticisms by Werts (1967).

Werts (1967), in a critique of the Holland-Richards work, proposed that, due to statistical artifacts, the actual degree of relationship between academic and nonacademic accomplishments is greater than the latter believed. The Holland-Richards approach relied upon the use of correlation coefficients for demonstrating lack of relationship between academic and nonacademic accomplishments. Werts pointed out, however, that the low frequencies with which the nonacademic attainments tend to occur will have the effect of depressing correlation coefficients even though the incidence of nonacademic accomplishments may be greater for those who are higher achievers academically. Such would be the case because the higher and the lower academic achievers both contain a majority of students who exhibit no accomplishments at all in nonacademic domains. The low correlation coefficients found by Holland and Richards thus reflect the point that most students fail to show nonacademic accomplishments regardless of their degree of academic achievement. But what of the minority who *do* show nonacademic accomplishments? How are they distributed across academic achievement levels? Werts found, in fact, that "A" students tended to show higher incidences of nonacademic accomplishments than "B" students, "B" students higher levels than "C" students, and so on, thus supporting his argument. While Holland and Richards (1967) in turn offered a rebuttal that contains some persuasive defenses for their position, most of the defenses hinge upon pointing to the relatively high proportions of nonacademic achievers whom one misses when selecting in terms of academic achievement. Such a line of discussion did not really refer itself to the point that *some* degree of relationship between academic and nonacademic accomplishments had been unearthed by Werts, and the linkages in question had been masked by the Holland-Richards use of correlation coefficients as their analytic technique.

There are, it seems to us, both substantive and methodological lessons to be derived from the Werts critique, and the present investigation was influenced by taking account of Werts in terms of each of these fronts. Substantively, it may be the case that the studies by the Holland-Richards group built in a certain degree of relationship between non-academic forms of accomplishment and the intellective realm they sought to assess by measuring the latter in terms of academic achievement indices rather than in terms of intelligence test results. To be sure, measures of intelligence and of academic achievement will be strongly correlated; as we have noted, academic achievement has constituted the validation criterion for intelligence tests. Nevertheless, intelligence indicators are expected to come closer to the level of sheer intellective ability than is information about academic accomplishment, thus reducing — although not necessarily eliminating — the extent to which motivation for achievement as such may bear upon the result. While academic achievement measures — whether grades or achievement test scores — are expected to reflect how much content the student has specifically learned in various academic areas and hence how vigorously he has applied himself, intelligence tests are expected to reflect ability or potential as distinct from content that has been mastered. The latter tests hence make minimal presuppositions concerning specific information that the respondent must have in hand at the time when he is assessed. Either the information that is needed is sufficiently general in character that its familiarity should be quite widespread — as when degree of clarity in understanding the words of one's native language is assayed; or the necessary information is supplied with the test — as when the postulates involved in some problem are presented and the respondent is asked to find the solution. Given an achievement motivation component in a person's level of academic accomplishment, we might expect a modicum of relationship with nonacademic forms of talented accomplishment to exist since the latter may also be influenced to some minor extent by the degree of achievement striving that characterizes the individual. Perhaps, then, the orthogonality which Holland and Richards sought, but as Werts showed, did not fully find between nonacademic forms of accomplishment and academic achievement, would be more closely approximated if we were to consider intelligence test scores instead of academic attainments.

In order to seek the kind of orthogonality mentioned, however, the methodological implication of Werts's discussion must be taken into account as well. Correlation coefficients cannot be counted on for providing an indication that two variables are unrelated to each other: a correlation coefficient may be near zero and still conceal a sizable degree of relationship when one of the variables concerns — as is the case with nonacademic forms of talented accomplishments — the relative incidence of events whose occurrence is rare in the first place. Rather, the type of analysis that seems indicated is to compare groups that are higher and lower regarding intelligence for their mean relative frequencies of one or another category of nonacademic accomplishments. If the means for the type of nonacademic accomplishments in question are the same for the higher and the lower intelligence groups, then we will know that the higher intelligence level is not associated with an enhanced degree of accomplishment in the nonacademic sphere under study. This would be analogous to finding in Werts's mode of analysis that, say, "A plus" students showed no greater incidence of attainments in, for example, creative writing, or social leadership, or the carrying out of extracurricular science projects, than did "B plus" students. What Werts actually found, on the other hand, was an incidence of accomplishments in such areas that was greater by a factor of one and one-half, two, or even occasionally four, when comparing the "A plus" with the "B plus" students. Would the same be true when comparing students of higher and lower intelligence levels? We shall report findings on this issue at length later in the book.

Assume for a moment that our first thesis could be sustained — that, within a college student sample, individual differences concerning general intelligence are quite unrelated to various indicators of talented accomplishments outside the academic arena, while at the same time exhibiting clear relationships to academic achievement itself. This is, of course, a negative thesis as far as nonacademic forms of talented accomplishments are concerned — that is, a proposition about what they are not related to. Even if intelligence were found to be linked with academic achievement, so that one could not argue that restriction of range concerning intelligence differences was acting to blur a linkage between intelligence and nonacademic accomplishments, it could still be plausibly maintained that the failure to find this linkage resulted from restriction of range concerning individual variation in nonacademic accomplishments. To show simply that there is *some* variation from one person to another regarding such accomplishments never can really answer this charge, for the critic can always come back with the reply: some, yes, but not enough. The definitive answer, therefore, is to be able to demonstrate that there is sufficient variation regarding these nonacademic forms of talented accomplishments to result in their linkage with another characteristic or characteristics which, on theoretical grounds, should be thus related — just as the definitive answer to the question of whether there is a sufficient range of intelligence differences is to show a relationship between intelligence and something else — in that instance, academic achievement. The second thesis of this book is to propose that individual differences in talented accomplishments outside the classroom, while not at all predictable from intelligence considerations, are related to a particular style of cognitive functioning that can be independently assessed. It is our aim to demonstrate that there *is* a way of defining how people deal cognitively with their world which, unlike the case with the cognitive abilities embraced by the intelligence concept, has the power to tell us something about who will be more likely and who less likely to exhibit various kinds of talented nonacademic accomplishments. What is the mode of cognitive functioning that forms the basis for this second thesis?

The term "creativity" conveys an aura of meaning in our everyday discourse that would seem, on the face of the matter, to be relevant for answering this question. Colloquially, we often use the word when trying to describe processes involved in talented accomplishment in such fields as writing, painting, scientific experimentation, music, or even the exercise of social leadership. Yet what we mean is hard to pin down — and perhaps appropriately so, since one is grappling here with the most distinctively human of man's characteristics. This ambiguity at the common-sense level, moreover, has been mirrored as well in the attempts of researchers in psychology and education to deal with the concept of creativity. Despite the burgeoning research literature which invokes the term, the search for viable psychological definitions of creativity has been fraught with pitfalls. This is not the place for exploring the paths and byways which have been pursued in that quest; the problem of disentangling the assessment of intelligence from the assessment of processes that may have relevance to creative aspects of human functioning has been discussed by, among others, Thorndike (1963a; 1963b) and Wallach and Kogan (1965), and an extensive literature review has recently been provided by Wallach (1969). What we shall do, however, is consider the major outlines that seem to emerge from this work, for they point in a consistent direction.

Various researchers have been concerned with trying to isolate forms of cognitive activity that might be meaningfully described as tapping creative roots in thought processes, as distinct from mere reflections of a person's level of general intelligence. From the literature review by Wallach (1969) can be derived the conclusion that some of these forms seem to be more independent of intelligence than others. Maximally independent of customarily defined intelligence have turned out to be characteristics of two sorts: a person's ability to generate a large number of ideas in response to a given task requirement, and his ability to produce in response to that task constraint many ideas that are unique in the sense that he stands relatively alone among his peers in suggesting them. From all indications, these two abilities are strongly related to each other, are pervasively exhibited across a wide range of situations, and are relatively independent of individual differences regarding general intelligence — at least across the span from medium to high intelligence levels. Let us consider first some of the evidence for these assertions, turn next to the issue of whether there seems to be any prima facie reason for viewing these abilities as possibly relevant to creativity in cognitive functioning, and then raise the question of validating such definitions of creative behavior against criteria of talented accomplishment.

Wallach and Kogan (1965) provided a demonstration of how individual differences in degree of productivity of ideas, and in the tendency to produce ideas that are unique, function as cognitive characteristics in a sample of fifth grade children (age 10–11 years). Consider the ways in which these abilities were measured — ways that take their origin from work by Guilford (see, for example, Guilford, 1959; 1964; 1967; and see also the review of research by Guilford and his collaborators provided in Wallach, 1969). Some tasks presented the person with conceptual entities, others, with visual materials. In the former category, one procedure —

"alternate uses" — named an object and asked the respondent to suggest for it as many uses as he could. Of the various objects named for this purpose, "a chair" was one, "a shoe" was another. The "similarities" procedure, another conceptual task, named pairs of objects — such as "milk and meat," or "cat and mouse," — and requested that the interviewee specify as many similarities as possible between the members of each pair. The visual tasks, in turn, presented the subject with various abstract visual designs or line forms. His job in each case was to generate as many interpretations as he could imagine concerning what each visual abstraction might represent. How were the two cognitive characteristics noted before measured from the responses to these procedures? Number of ideas produced simply referred, in the case of each task, to how many suggestions the child made in responding to any request — for instance, how many uses he could suggest for a shoe. The other characteristic that we noted, namely, the uniqueness of the suggested ideas, referred to the number of one-of-a-kind suggestions that the child offered in response to each request on a given task — that is, the number of suggestions made that were offered by no one else in the sample of children as a response to the same request. In responding to the request for similarities between milk and meat, for example, one of the unique suggestions offered was "they are government-inspected," while "they come from animals" was a suggestion offered by many children. With some measures in hand for evaluating individual differences in number of ideas and in number of unique ideas generated in response to a task request, what results were obtained concerning the consistency of these characteristics across kinds of tasks, concerning their relationship with each other, and concerning their relationship with intelligence?

The findings were quite clear-cut and identical for children of both sexes. Number of ideas and number of unique ideas were highly consistent regardless of the type of task. Whether asking for suggestions as to what a visual design might connote, what similarities link a train and a tractor, or what uses a newspaper might be put to, for example, children who offered many ideas in one task setting offered many ideas in the other task settings as well, while children offering few ideas in one case offered comparably few ideas across the board. Analogous findings prevailed for uniqueness of ideas: number of unique ideas suggested was consistently high or low for different children regardless of task context. What of the relationship between number and uniqueness of ideas? The two indices were strongly correlated, indicating that the person who offered many ideas also provided a large quantity of unique suggestions among them. The reason for this relationship was not far to seek, for it already was clear from earlier work (see, for example, Christensen, Guilford, and Wilson, 1957) that ideas of greater uniqueness or un-commonness come later in a sequence of emitted ideas, while those of greater commonness or familiarity come earlier. When faced with a task such as naming uses for an object, common uses will tend to be thought of first, unique ones only if the person keeps generating ideational possibilities. Consider, finally, the issue of relationships with general intelligence. Both number and uniqueness of ideas proved to be essentially independent of various indices of intelligence. Within at least the range from medium to high levels of intelligence, which was essentially the range represented by this sample of children, number and uniqueness of ideas produced were hardly at all reflecting greater or lesser degrees of general intelligence. This finding is of some surprise value since we might well expect verbal facility and reasoning ability to aid performance not only on intelligence tests but also on tests concerning the types of ideational functioning just described.

Given the strong linkage found between number and uniqueness of ideas, we find ourselves facing an interpretational problem when we seek a psychological account of what may underlie individual differences in these characteristics. Is the basic mechanism an urge for uniqueness, with those who possess high degrees of this urge impelled to produce large quantities of ideas because that is the means whereby they can reach the unique ones? Or is the basic mechanism concerned with cognitive energy level in the sense that some people simply show more ideational activity than others? On this latter view, the production of unique ideas would merely be a byproduct of generating a larger number of ideas, since as the size of the output increases, so also does the likelihood of suggesting ideas of greater uniqueness. Nor is there any reason in principle why both hypothetical mechanisms — urge for uniqueness and cognitive energy level — might not operate jointly. At any rate, either mechanism would seem to possess a modicum of face validity as relevant for what we might want to mean psychologically by creativity. But more on this matter later. First let us document, a bit more extensively, the case for viewing number and uniqueness of ideas as individual-difference characteristics that are pervasive, related to each other, and independent of intelligence.

Wallach and Kogan (1965) believed that their finding of little or no relationship between number and uniqueness of ideas on the one hand and intelligence on the other, depended specifically upon administering the ideational flow tasks in a situation of freedom from such testlike pressures as the provision of time limits and group administration in a classroom. While such factors may maximize this independence of the ideational output and uniqueness measures from intelligence (see, for example, Boersma and O'Bryan, 1968, for positive findings on this point, but Kogan and Morgan, 1967, for a more ambiguous outcome), further consideration of relevant evidence suggests that the independence in question is more robust than that. A high degree of independence has been demonstrated even when tasks concerning ideational flow have been administered in relatively pressured, testlike circumstances. These results actually offer further testimony to the pervasiveness of the ideational output and uniqueness characteristics on which we have focused. The studies that we next pass in review ran the gamut from relatively free to relatively pressured in their administration contexts for ideational flow tasks.

Let us first move down the age range from the fifth-grade level represented in the Wallach-Kogan work, and then sample some research at higher ages. Ward (1968), with 7- to 8-year-old children, found essentially the same picture as emerged from the Wallach-Kogan research. Even with a sample of preschoolers, Ward (1968) obtained results that were sufficiently comparable — although not the same in all respects — as to suggest that number and uniqueness of ideas already exist in the very young child as individual-difference characteristics that are linked to each other and are distinct from intelligence. A strong hint in the same direction already was available, furthermore, in earlier work by Gewirtz (1948a; 1948b) and Bereiter (1961) where, with children of about 5 to 6 years of age, such indices of ideational output as naming as many objects as possible and describing one's house as fully as possible turned out to be related to one another and independent of intelligence. A recent study of 6-year-olds by Orpet and Meyers (1966) makes the same point again.

Moving up the age scale, consider an investigation by McGuire, Hindsman, King, and Jennings (1961) using seventh graders as subjects. The number that a child could envision of possible consequences arising from various proposed changes and of problems arising from various common situations were found to relate to each other and to stand relatively apart from intelligence. With students ranging from 11 to 15 years in age, Clark, Veldman, and Thorpe (1965) measured the number of statistically unique ideas offered in response to such tasks as those just described from the McGuire, and others work, and obtained no linkage with intelligence test scores. So also, May and Metcalf (1965) found measures of ideational output to cohere strongly among themselves and to be independent of intelligence for a sample of eighth graders. Similar results for a sample of seventh and eighth graders were reported by Feldhusen, Denny, and Condon (1965). Garwood (1964), in turn, found for college students that number of uses listed for common objects correlated strongly with number of uses suggested that were fully unique in the sense that only one member of the sample offered the use in question for a given object. Analogously, number of consequences named as possible results of various proposed changes correlated strongly in the Garwood study with the number of these suggested consequences that were unusual ones. With the effects of intelligence partialled out, note too that Barron (1955, 1957, 1963) obtained evidence for his young adult subjects of a residual dimension of individual differences defined by a repertoire of behaviors related to number and uniqueness of ideas. The dimension in question was defined by such measures as the relative uniqueness of uses suggested by the respondent on a task requesting the naming of uses for objects, the unusualness of the consequences imagined when thinking about what would happen if certain changes suddenly took place, the extensiveness of the range of ideas discerned by the subject in considering sets of varied objects and properties, and a rating of the person as carried out by psychologists after a several-day observation period for fluency of ideas.

In general, then, considerable evidence points down the same road as the Wallach-Kogan research. Ideational fluency and fluency-dependent forms of uniqueness of ideas seem to define individual-difference characteristics that have relatively little to do with intelligence. Before going on to consider why these characteristics seem suggestive in regard to creativity, however, there is a technical point that needs mention concerning the linkage between them. It is somewhat difficult on technical grounds to document the degree of relationship between the number of ideas offered in response to a given task and the number of such ideas that are statistically unique. Claims that the two characteristics are in fact empirically linked thus have to be made with due caution. The reason for this difficulty is that the person who produces a larger supply of unique ideas will by that fact also be producing a larger total output of ideas. The result is that the two measures have to be related in some degree simply because the former will be a component of the latter. One answer to this issue is to compare the number of statistically unique ideas produced on one task with the total number of ideas produced on another, since in this manner the two measures are no longer contaminated by derivation from the same stream of ideational content. When we follow this procedure in, say, the Garwood study mentioned before, the degree of linkage between number and uniqueness of ideas still remains quite powerful. Another approach is to compare the number of statistically unique ideas produced on a task with the remaining number of nonunique ideas produced on the same task — on the assumption that the latter index still provides an approximation to the total number of ideas generated. With unique ideas removed from the measure of ideational output in this manner, output and uniqueness levels on a given task still remain strongly correlated in, for example, the Wallach-Kogan research. Such considerations make clear, then, that the relationship obtained between number and uniqueness of ideas produced by a person is not just a computational artifact.

A genuine link thus exists between magnitude of ideational output and the incidence of unique ideas among the total — a link reflecting the fact that common ideas come earlier and uncommon ones later in a stream of generated ideas. With number and uniqueness of ideas both in turn found to be minimally related to general intelligence, we seem to have in hand two prime candidates for describing creativity in cognitive functioning. Each offers a possible mechanism — cognitive energy level and urge for uniqueness, respectively — which, as we noted before, conveys an aura of suitability when it comes to hypothesizing what creativity might signify in psychological terms. Next we will consider for a moment where this aura of face validity seems to come from. Then, since face validity may be deceptive and at any rate is never sufficient, we will turn to the issue of criterion validity — that is, the issue which defines our second thesis: do the characteristics here considered help us predict who will show various forms of talented accomplishment and who will not?

To return first to face validity. A ready flow of ideas — the freedom to generate extensive ideational possibilities — has been described as important for their work in many introspective accounts provided by various eminent practitioners in the arts and sciences. To take just one example, the poet Dryden has described his writing efforts as involving production of ". . . a confus'd Mass of Thoughts, tumbling over one another in the Dark" (Ghiselin, 1955, p. 80). In more recent times, the ever-increasing awareness found in Western culture concerning the importance of innovation and change as distinct from maintenance of traditional conceptions in almost every field of artistic, scientific, and even mathematical activity has inevitably brought in its wake a focusing of attention upon envisioning the possible. To imagine what is possible is to produce many ideas and to find among them ones that are unusual in a way that suggests new meanings or interpretations that may be relevant. It is only through generating ideational possibilities that, for example, non-Euclidean geometries or non-Aristotelian logics could be evolved: alternatives to ideational systems firmly anchored in tradition had to be entertained. Something analogous was going on when new theories were constructed as competitors to the old in the recent growth spurt experienced in almost every branch of empirical science; and also when, in the arts, Schoenberg constructed a new set of harmonic assumptions for composing music; cubist painters tore apart familiar objects and placed their components into new juxtapositions based on new principles of visual order; or John Cage undid the traditional structure of the piano and formed it instead into a musical instrument possessing a quite different set of sound characteristics than before.

If even Dryden could readily sense the importance of an unruly, cascading flow of ideas in the nourishment of his poetry writing, how much more important has this become in the time since, with its increasingly greater emphasis upon the generating of new thought forms. In the visual arts, for example, the last few centuries have witnessed an almost complete transformation in the role of the artist from an artisan who in principle operated almost exclusively within tradition-dictated rules to an inventor who feels free to experiment at will regarding ways of utilizing the materials from his environment toward aesthetic ends. Most likely it is this very growth of ideational freedom itself in the arts and sciences which has been responsible for our present epoch's ability to formulate an explicit concern with creativity as a detachable conceptual entity. The generating of ideational alternatives, as distinct from the following of traditional or customary forms, thus stands at the very center of what the society means by a term such as creativity. What, in turn, must the generating of cognitive possibilities look like if one observes a presumably creative person at work? It must take the form of producing a large ideational output, this large number of generated ideas also eventuating by that fact in the production of a large number of relatively unique ones as well.

The foregoing considerations indicate that it is not at all difficult to muster face validity for defining creativity in terms of the number and the uniqueness of the ideas that a person is able to generate. Since, as we have noted, the presence of a more extensive ideational flow guarantees the emergence of greater uniqueness, we are left with two different, but not necessarily mutually exclusive, ways of viewing what is happening psychologically — depending upon whether we take the number of ideas produced or the uniqueness of the produced ideas as the primary datum. Recall our earlier distinction between cognitive energy level and urge for uniqueness as names for the two hypothetical mechanisms that suggest themselves. If we take variation in the number of ideas a person generates to be pivotal, then we are led to think of differences in level of ideational activity or cognitive energy as the essence of the matter, with unique ideas arising as an epiphenomenal result of producing more ideas. If, on the other hand, we consider variation in ideational uniqueness to be the main issue, then we are led to think in terms of degree of urge for uniqueness as the heart of our interpretation, with a larger number of ideas poured forth because this is the way a person will hit upon those of greater uniqueness. In number and uniqueness of produced ideas, we hence have a definition of cognitive functioning that may help account for who will display stronger talented accomplishments outside the classroom. And in cognitive energy level and urge for uniqueness, we have two possible interpretations that may help clarify what the style of cognitive functioning in question is about psychologically.

Now we are in a position to flesh out what our second thesis requires us to demonstrate. The mode of cognitive functioning that we believe will provide some leverage in predicting talented forms of nonacademic accomplishments is the dimension of individual differences concerning productivity and uniqueness of ideational content which has been found in such research as that by Wallach and Kogan (1965) to stand relatively independent of a person's intelligence level. Since productivity and uniqueness of ideas will necessarily be correlated, however, we can never tell simply from a person's standing on this dimension whether ideational output as such (and hence cognitive energy level) or producing unique ideas in particular (and hence an urge for uniqueness) is the more responsible psychological agent for any obtained relationships with nonacademic accomplishments. To disentangle these possibilities, therefore, we will want to carry out our inquiry with persons who are high or low in ideational output regardless of the uniqueness of their ideas, and with persons who are high or low in ideational uniqueness regardless of the number of ideas they produce. Perhaps number and uniqueness of ideas are so highly correlated that this separation will have no effect; but perhaps, on the other hand, emphasis upon number versus uniqueness of ideas will turn out to have quite different consequences for linkages with talented attainments in the nonacademic environment. In all of this, we are seeking to obtain criterion validation concerning promising candidates for defining aspects of cognitive functioning that are different from intelligence and that may be relevant to the creativity concept.

To succeed in establishing such criterion validity would accomplish two things. First, it would advance our substantive understanding of the cognitive underpinnings on which various forms of talented nonacademic attainments are built. We would learn something about thought styles implicated in talented accomplishments encountered outside of school. It may well turn out, furthermore, that the same thought style forms a predisposing factor that may lead one person toward excelling at a science project, another toward extensive involvement in creative writing, and a third toward painting pictures. At issue may be cognitive wellsprings, if you will, that can eventuate in alternative forms of expressive acts. Such, indeed, is what we would expect if something of any degree of generality can be said concerning how talented people grapple cognitively with their environment.

But there is also a very practical type of aim that we feel would be furthered by establishing the kind of criterion validity under discussion. To the extent that we find intelligence telling us nothing about a variety of forms of talented nonacademic accomplishment but also find a different category of cognitive information enlightening in this regard, we will have strengthened the case for a liberalized view of human talent — a view that emphasizes diversity rather than homogeneity in the means for selecting talented persons. For we will have shown that, while intelligence differences among college students may predict grades, undeniably valuable forms of talented contributions which do not earn grades for the student fall completely through the net provided by intelligence tests but are captured in some degree by other kinds of cognitive data concerning the student. Since there is no doubt that the talented nonacademic accomplishments into which we shall inquire are useful to society, we have no choice but to concern ourselves with how to select students who display them. We will have learned that intelligence tests cannot help us here and should not be used with the expectation that they can be of aid. Rather, the implication will be that we should utilize direct signs of the talented accomplishments as the best clues to future displays of similar attainments, and perhaps also that we should seek to evaluate the intelligence-free aspects of cognitive functioning that may predispose a student toward such accomplishments in general.

In summary, then, the theses that we hope to establish are as follows, and we mean them to apply within the general range of intelligence defined by a college student population. (a) While individual differences regarding intelligence level will relate to customary criteria of academic achievement, intelligence differences will be quite unrelated to degree of talented accomplishment in each of a variety of pursuits outside the formal classroom situation. Among the pursuits in question are, for example, painting, creative writing, and the exercise of social leadership. (b) In contrast to intelligence, degree of ideational productivity and the uniqueness of the ideas produced define a mode of cognitive functioning which will be related to the display of talented nonacademic accomplishments. Responsible for this connection may be the ideational productivity aspect, the uniqueness aspect, or both.

Chapter 2

Number of Ideas,
Uniqueness of Ideas,
and Intelligence

The first step that we must take in order to evaluate our
theses is to replicate for the sample of students in our research
the relative independence already demonstrated elsewhere
between ideational productivity and uniqueness, on the one
hand, and general intelligence, on the other. This we shall
do in the present chapter. The materials considered will also
permit us to determine for our sample the degree of relationship between the two ideational indices — productivity
and uniqueness. We recall that earlier findings indicated
this relationship to be considerable. To find the ideational
and the intelligence measures in turn more or less independent
of one another would provide a clear warrant for proceeding
to determine whether they are distinguishable in their linkage
with talented nonacademic accomplishments. If they should
not be independent to at least a moderate degree, the likelihood of finding them differentially related to outside criteria
would be reduced from the outset.

Our study concerned a volunteer sample of 503 students from a recent incoming freshman class at Duke. They were recruited on the basis of their willingness to take the time to provide us with information requested from them in a mailing sent during the summer preceding their arrival on campus. Our aim was to lean over backward toward indicating that we wanted them to return the information only if they really wished to do so. While our motivation for proceeding this way was based in part on ethical considerations, we also felt that the psychologically soundest strategy was to insure that our sample contained only persons who were interested in providing the data for which they were asked, rather than including as well persons who would reply only grudgingly or with feelings of malice toward the investigators. This goal meant providing the student with as much assurance as possible to the effect that his choosing to respond or not to respond would not be used in any way against him. Our letter to each student hence included the following points:

> In the enclosed booklet, you will find a number of tasks. To be quite frank, these are not 'personality tests' of any kind. Also, they are not academic tests. The responses you make will not be used to evaluate you academically in any way by anybody. Your responses will be kept strictly confidential by the researchers. These tasks, not you, are under test. After you have had a chance to look over the instructions and tasks, decide whether you would consider filling out the booklet an invasion of your privacy; if you feel that it would be, do not return the booklet.

Among the materials placed before the students were the procedures that would permit us to measure ideational productivity and uniqueness. No time limit was suggested; rather, the students were urged to take as much time over the tasks as they felt they needed in order to satisfy themselves with the answers they provided. The implication, given the amount of materials involved, was that anywhere from one hour to three or more hours might be consumed in responding. Accordingly, our request that the student participate only if he wished to do so was far from gratuitous. He would have to expend a goodly amount of time and effort if he took us up on our invitation. Approximately 40 percent of the freshman class agreed to participate on these terms.

The sample of 503 consisted of 302 men and 201 women. From our perspective, however, the presence of both sexes in the sample is not of direct psychological moment. Our theses have not been framed in sex-specific terms; rather, we expect them to apply to members of either sex, and we have no particular reason to believe that one sex will provide clearer confirmation of our hypotheses than the other. While the presentation of our results hence will emphasize chiefly the entire sample without regard to sex of respondents, we shall present some findings by sex as well in order to demonstrate that the results are indeed analogous for the two sexes.

Intelligence was measured in a very conventional manner — by using the respondents' scores on the verbal and mathematical parts of the Scholastic Aptitude Test (SAT; College Entrance Examination Board, 1966). This standard intelligence instrument was taken by them at least once during their senior year of high school and, by many of them, during their junior year as well — the test content itself, of course, differing on each administration. The verbal and mathematical aptitude sections of this test constitute oft-used prognosticators for predicting how well a student may be expected to do in his college grades. In order to maximize the reliability of measuring each of the two forms of intellective aptitude, the scores from all occasions of measurement were combined and a weighted average for each student was obtained. The weighting process gave greater emphasis to senior year than to junior year administrations and also made an adjustment for test familiarity. Verbal and mathematical scores were kept separate in this averaging. The rules for the averaging procedure were those devised by the test makers (College Entrance Examination Board, 1966) and can be summarized as follows: if the student took the SAT once in the senior year, the resulting scores were used directly; if he took the SAT twice in the senior year, the scores were added, divided by 2, and 5 subtracted from the result; if he took it three times in the senior year, the scores were added, divided by 3, and 10 subtracted from the result; if he took it once in the junior year and once in the senior year, the senior-year scores were doubled, added to the junior-year scores, and divided by 3; if he took it once in the junior year and twice in the senior year, the scores were added, divided by 3, and 5 subtracted from the result; and finally, if he took it twice in the junior year and once in the senior year, the senior-year scores were quadrupled, added to the sum of the junior-year scores, divided by 6, and 10 subtracted from the result. From applying these rules, therefore, a pair of scores was obtained for each student reflecting the most reliable estimate available of his verbal and mathematical aptitude levels.

Our aim, in turn, was to obtain a single best estimate of each student's general intelligence. Accordingly, we converted all verbal and mathematical scores into standard score form as based upon the data for the entire sample — that is, equally weighted transformations — and then added the two standard scores in order to obtain a single index of overall intellective aptitude. It is common procedure to add the verbal and mathematical SAT scores when a measure of overall intelligence is desired, and this procedure is supported by the fact that the test scores are known to be correlated to a substantial degree.

Can we say something about the general intelligence level of our sample in absolute terms? Using the calibrating system provided by the makers of the SAT, the means for the 502 students on whom SAT scores were available were 619.12 (SD = 70.12) on the verbal section and 644.88 (SD = 69.23) on the mathematical section. Since each section is scaled in such a way as to yield a score range extending from 200 to 800 with a mean set at about 500 for those high school seniors who take the test, we are talking about college students who fall within the upper half of the overall score distribution on the SAT. Some expectable sex differences in the patterning of the verbal and mathematical scores were obtained, with the females scoring much higher than the males (about 40 points) on verbal aptitude and somewhat lower than the males (about 17 points) on mathematical aptitude. Both differences were statistically significant by t tests, the verbal aptitude score difference quite strongly so. The data are shown in Table 2.1. Note also, by the way, that our volunteer sample turned out to be highly similar in their verbal and mathematical SAT scores to that year's freshman class as a whole — whether taking the class as a unit (verbal score mean = 615 and SD = 74; mathematical score mean = 642 and SD = 70) or considering each sex separately. No volunteer bias with regard to intelligence was operating, therefore, in the selecting of students for our sample.

TABLE 2.1

Verbal and Mathematical Scholastic Aptitude
Test Scores for the Members of the Sample

	Verbal		Mathematical	
	Mean	SD	Mean	SD
Entire sample (N = 502)	619.12	70.12	644.88	69.23
Men (N = 302)	603.32	71.32	651.69	67.38
Women (N = 200)	642.98	61.10	634.60	70.88

Note — The N comprises all members of the sample for whom SAT scores were available.

The sex difference found in SAT scores — particularly the large difference in favor of the women on verbal aptitude — reveal that we will want to define a student's intelligence level relative to the distribution for his sex when it comes time to compare higher and lower intelligence persons regarding other criteria. That is, our higher intelligence group will consist of men who are high among the men and women who are high among the women on intelligence, while our lower intelligence group will analogously consist of men who are low among the men and women who are low among the women regarding intelligence. If we did not take sex of respondent into account in this manner, the strong bias toward women in the verbal aptitude scores would result in the higher intelligence group ending up with disproportionately more women and fewer men than the lower intelligence group. Aligning a difference in the proportion of men and women with a difference in level of intelligence could well cause interpretational ambiguity, since a confounding of intelligence level with the sex of the respondent would occur.

Next we turn to the measurement of number and uniqueness of ideas. Both characteristics were assessed from data provided in response to the same procedures. These procedures, four in number, were derived from the Wallach-Kogan (1965) research mentioned earlier. All four were expected on the basis of that work to provide equally relevant materials from which the cognitive dispositions of interest to us could be evaluated. The aim of including several probes was simply to increase reliability of measurement by sampling a diverse range of task stimuli whose ideational responses would vary both in number and in relative uniqueness for different individuals. Two tasks, which we may call "uses" and "similarities," involved verbal stimulus materials. The other two, which we may call "pattern meanings" and "line meanings," confronted the subject with visual stimulus materials. The verbal and visual procedures were alternated in their presentation to the student, appearing in his booklet in the following order: uses, pattern meanings, similarities, line meanings. Here is what the student read about the respective tasks.

The student began his work with the following instructions concerning the uses task:

> On each of these pages will appear the name of a familiar object. We would like you to write down all the different ways you can think of in which the object might be used. Do not hesitate to write down whatever ways you can think of in which the object might be used as long as they are possible uses for the object that is named.

The first object named was "a newspaper"; the second, "an automobile tire — either the tube or the outer tire"; and the third, "a shoe." Each was listed on the top of a fresh sheet of blank 8 1/2 by 11 in. paper, with the reverse side of each sheet also available for writing down further ideas if the student was so inclined. Similar practices were followed for the other tasks as well. After the three pages devoted to the uses task came instructions for the pattern-meanings procedure:

> On each of these pages will appear a pattern of a particular sort. We would like you to write down all the different things you can think of that each complete pattern might suggest. You can turn the pattern around any way you like. Do not hesitate to write down whatever things you can think of, as long as they are possible things that the pattern might suggest.

On the top of each of three blank sheets appeared one of the patterns displayed in the first row of Figure 1. These abstract forms simply served to provide representationally ambiguous visual materials that would be open to numerous alternative interpretations. Following the pages containing these patterns, the student read instructions for the similarities task:

FIGURE 1   **Top,** pattern-meanings task items.   **Bottom,** line-meanings task items.

On each of these pages will appear the names of two objects. We would like you to write down all the different ways you can think of in which the two objects might be alike. Do not hesitate to write down whatever ways you can think of in which the two objects might be alike, as long as they are possible similarities between the objects.

The pairs of objects listed on the top of successive blank sheets were, first, "a potato and a carrot," second, "a train and a tractor," and third, "a grocery store and a restaurant." Finally, there followed the instructions for the line-meanings procedure:

On each of these pages will appear a continuous line of a particular sort. We would like you to write down all the different things you can think of that each complete line might suggest. You can turn the line around any way you like. Do not hesitate to write down whatever things you can think of, as long as they are possible things that the line might suggest.

In the second row of Figure 1 will be found the three lines that appeared on the top of successive blank sheets of the booklet. They served to increase further the range of visual stimuli for which construals as to possible meanings were requested. In this manner, samplings of visual as well as verbal starting points were provided for assessing the plenitude and unusualness of the student's flow of ideas. Next we must consider how, in more detail, these measurements were derived.

The first type of measure, number of ideas, hardly needs further explication. We simply counted, in the case of each of the three items comprising each of the four tasks, the number of ideas which the student wrote down. With unlimited time and as much space as both sides of a standard sheet of paper would provide, the student had relatively wide latitude for generating as many ideas as he wished.

But how did we assess uniqueness of ideas? Through counting, again for each item on each task, those of a student's ideas that were fully unique in the sense that he was the only member of the sample of 503 who thought of the given idea as a response to the item in question. As it turns out, such a rule is much easier to state in the abstract than to put into practice. Ambiguities arise concerning whether two ideas offered by different individuals as uses for a shoe, for example, *really* should be considered different — and hence potentially unique if no one else in the sample turned out to think of either one — or rather should be judged equivalent and hence nonunique. It did not seem reasonable, for example, to consider synonymous terms such as "toy" and "plaything" or related modifiers such as "usually peeled" and "always peeled" as referring to different ideas rather than to the same idea. Hence, a manual had to be written instructing judges about what we deemed to be superficial differences that would not qualify ideas for the distinction of being considered different from one another. In brief, the manual's intent was to spell out some principles for deciding when a verbal difference between responses was simply a matter of mode of expression rather than of a difference in ideas. To make clear, therefore, what was *not* used as a basis for judging an idea to be unique, here follow the main principles contained in the manual:

(*a*) Different terms which have the same meaning are considered to be the same. For example, "toy" and "plaything" are categorized as the same use for a shoe.

(*b*) Singular and plural responses are considered to be the same in the case of the verbal items. For instance, "line garbage can" and "line garbage cans" are categorized as the same use for a newspaper. In the case of the visual items, on the other hand, singular and plural responses are not considered to be the same because different images are involved: the student envisions a different percept in each case.

(*c*) Such phrases as "part of," "piece of," or "article of," are treated as irrelevant when they refer to a collective concept. For example, "piece of string" and "string" are categorized as the same response for the second item in the line meanings task. The aforementioned kind of phrases are retained as meaningful, however, when they refer to a discrete concept, because different images are envisioned. For instance, "part of a racetrack" and "racetrack" are categorized as different responses for the second item in the pattern meanings task.

(*d*) References to the position of the viewer are treated as irrelevant. For instance, "upside-down vase" and "vase" are classified as the same response for the third item in the line meanings task.

(*e*) Qualifiers representing varying degrees of endorsement are considered to be the same. For example, in relation to similarities between a potato and a carrot, the following responses are taken as equivalent: "always peeled," "usually peeled," "often peeled," "normally peeled," "sometimes peeled," and "peeled." Analogously, qualifiers representing varying degrees of nonendorsement are considered to be the same. For instance, the following responses are taken as equivalent similarities for train and tractor: "never colored white," "seldom colored white," and "not colored white."

While it is well and good to have the aforementioned principles, one must be able to demonstrate an acceptable level of agreement in their application to the streams of ideas written down by the subjects. As a reliability check, two independent judges scored all the ideational responses in 20 randomly selected protocols as unique or nonunique. In the case of each item on each procedure — hence, 12 items in all — we calculated the number of responses upon which the judges agreed in their assignment of unique or nonunique status, divided by the total number of responses given to the item. As Table 2.2 indicates, the percentage of responses on which the judges agreed in their classifications of unique or nonunique was satisfactorily high for the various items. For all the data combined, 84 percent agreement was demonstrated. For the data on the verbal and the visual items taken separately, the respective agreement levels were 81 percent and 88 percent. Thus assured of sufficient reliability in the making of decisions about the uniqueness or nonuniqueness of an ideational response, responsibility in applying the manual's principles was assigned to a single judge, a second judge then resolving any instances about which the first judge felt doubtful.

There was no reason in principle, of course, why uniqueness of ideas was assessed in terms of the number of ideas that were fully unique, rather than including also, for example, ideas that were common to only two members of the sample, or that were suggested by no more than three members. The definition of uniqueness is a partially arbitrary matter, in that an idea proposed by two people in our sample of 503 might have been proposed by only one person in another sample of 250. Our concern, therefore, is with relative uniqueness within a given sample. There was a reason

TABLE 2.2

Percentage of Agreements between Two Independent Judges
in Classifying Ideas as Unique and Nonunique
for a Random Sample of 20 Protocols

Task and item	Total number of responses	Percentage of agreements
Uses		
1	256	80
2	121	79
3	112	80
Pattern meanings		
1	99	91
2	103	83
3	71	87
Similarities		
1	135	88
2	150	87
3	109	73
Line meanings		
1	107	90
2	86	85
3	116	91

in practice, on the other hand, for restricting our definition of uniqueness to number of one-of-a-kind responses. Recall that we wished to compare the psychological implications of ideational output and ideational uniqueness, since the two cognitive characteristics suggested different underlying mechanisms. Hence, an approach was needed that would maximize the potential separation between the two. By defining uniqueness in terms of the number of fully unique responses, we provided as much of an opportunity as possible for the uniqueness count to diverge from the measure of total number of ideas produced. The more we had relaxed our definition of uniqueness, in other words, the larger would have become the proportion of the total number of ideas represented by the sub-set of those ideas that we were categorizing as relatively unique. A restrictive definition of uniqueness gave us as much of a chance as possible to measure something different from what we already were tapping by simply counting the number of ideas which the person generated.

TABLE 2.3

Percentage of Total Number of Ideas Classified as Unique for the Members of the Sample

Task and item	Total number of responses	Percentage unique
Uses		
1	6932	6
2	3650	9
3	3499	10
Pattern meanings		
1	2986	36
2	2825	29
3	2027	35
Similarities		
1	3544	5
2	3312	4
3	2870	6
Line meanings		
1	2964	14
2	2346	26
3	2866	16

Note — Data based on $N = 503$.

How small a proportion of the total ideational output did the fully unique ideas in fact turn out to be? Table 2.3 indicates that we experienced a relatively good degree of success in this regard. The percentages of total ideas produced that were fully unique ranged for the various items from a low of 4 percent to a high of 36 percent. In general, the visual items yielded a larger proportion of unique responses than the verbal items. We can conclude, then, that the unique ideas represented a sufficiently small sub-set of the total number of ideas to permit our entertaining the notion that two psychologically different characteristics were under examination — despite the fact that we still would expect them to be substantially related.

Before proceeding to consider the relationships between intelligence, on the one hand, and the indicators of ideational output and uniqueness, on the other, we must document our assumption that the various task materials used for assessing number and uniqueness of ideas function in a generally similar manner. This documentation, in turn, requires that a prior question also be examined — namely, whether the three items comprising each task themselves yielded similar results. The first question, then, is whether a person generating many ideas or many unique ideas on one item of a given task also tends to do so on the other two items — that is, the internal consistency of each task. Tables 2.4 through 2.7 present data indicating that the answer is yes. Shown are the sample-wide correlations between number of ideas on each pair of items in the set of three, and between number of unique ideas on each pair of items in the set of three for each of the tasks that were administered — uses, pattern meanings, similarities, and line meanings. The generally high correlations obtained signify that, within a given procedure — such as uses or line meanings — a student who offers many ideas in response to one item also is inclined to do so in response to the others. Likewise, if a student presents many unique ideas when con-

TABLE 2.4

*Correlations among Items for Number and Uniqueness
of Ideas on the Uses Task*

Item pairs	Number	Uniqueness
1 *vs.* 2	.73	.52
1 *vs.* 3	.70	.49
2 *vs.* 3	.72	.62

Note — Data based on $N = 503$.

TABLE 2.5

*Correlations among Items for Number and Uniqueness
of Ideas on the Pattern-Meanings Task*

Item pairs	Number	Uniqueness
1 *vs.* 2	.76	.61
1 *vs.* 3	.75	.66
2 *vs.* 3	.77	.62

Note — Data based on $N = 503$.

TABLE 2.6

*Correlations among Items for Number and Uniqueness
of Ideas on the Similarities Task*

Item pairs	Number	Uniqueness
1 *vs.* 2	.72	.44
1 *vs.* 3	.72	.29
2 *vs.* 3	.77	.52

Note — Data based on $N = 503$.

fronted with one item, he will tend to do the same when
confronted with the other items as well. The data for each
sex considered separately were analogous to those for the

TABLE 2.7

Correlations among Items for Number and Uniqueness
of Ideas on the Line-Meanings Task

Item pairs	Number	Uniqueness
1 vs. 2	.71	.53
1 vs. 3	.73	.54
2 vs. 3	.75	.54

Note — Data based on $N = 503$.

sample as a whole. So much, then, for the matter of consistency within a task. What about consistency across the tasks?

In Table 2.8 are presented the answers to this question both for number of ideas produced and for number of unique ideas produced. The entries above the diagonal show the sample-wide correlations between all pairs of the four tasks for the total number of ideas generated in responding to a task. The entries below the diagonal present the analogous material in the case of the total number of unique ideas produced in the course of responding to a task. For both

TABLE 2.8

Correlations among Tasks for Total Number of Ideas
and Total Unique Ideas on Each Task

	Uses	Pattern meanings	Similarities	Line meanings
Uses		.59	.71	.57
Pattern meanings	.43		.68	.79
Similarities	.51	.49		.67
Line meanings	.38	.70	.37	

Note — Entries for total number of ideas appear above diagonal; entries for total unique ideas appear below diagonal. Data based on the 502 members of the sample for whom SAT scores were available.

measures, the correlations are high — although they are somewhat higher for output than for uniqueness. Whatever the kind of task material that one uses for prodding a person into providing an idea sequence concerning a given topic, persons show consistency with themselves, and differences from others, both in their output of ideas and in the extent to which they muster ideas that are unique. As before, separate analyses by sex yielded similar results. We may conclude, then, that in the case of ideational output or ideational uniqueness, the four tasks provide roughly comparable types of assessment. What they have in common, therefore, should give us a single best estimate of a person's typical level of productivity or uniqueness regarding his flow of ideas. Now we can turn to the issue of relationships between such measures and intelligence.

Whether considering verbal or mathematical SAT scores as the intelligence estimate, we find from Table 2.9

TABLE 2.9

Correlations between Ideational and Intellective Measures

	SAT verbal	SAT mathematical
Number of ideas		
Uses	.08	—.02
Pattern meanings	.03	—.07
Similarities	.03	—.03
Line meanings	.08	—.05
Uniqueness of ideas		
Uses	.08	.05
Pattern meanings	.05	—.03
Similarities	.03	—.03
Line meanings	.09	—.03

Note — Data based on the 502 members of the sample for whom SAT scores were available.

that the sample-wide correlations between the measures of ideational characteristics and intelligence are uniformly low. Similar results again obtain for each sex considered separately. The verbal and mathematical SAT scores, in turn, were correlated .38 for the sample as a whole and to a comparable degree for each sex considered separately. Thus, the correlation between the two intelligence estimates is highly significant and substantially greater than any of the correlations in Table 2.9, which average out to approximately zero. Considering this information together with the information of Table 2.8, which indicates that whether we concern ourselves with output or with uniqueness of ideas, diverse measures intercorrelate substantially as well — we can conclude that the present results provide a clear replication of the Wallach-Kogan findings concerning the basic separation from intelligence of the two ideational characteristics under study. Asking a person to tell us his ideas about something seems to elicit cognitive phenomena that have very little dependence upon how bright or dull he is in a general-intelligence sense — at least in the upper ranges of intelligence represented by our sample. Whether his flow of ideas will be extensive or restricted cannot be guessed with much success from knowing his intelligence level. Analogously, whether many or few unique ideas will be found among those that he offers is equally unfathomable from information about intelligence. Whatever productivity and uniqueness of ideas may signify psychologically, then, they have little to do with intelligence in an above-average group.

But do number and uniqueness of ideas have anything to do with each other? As Table 2.10 indicates, the answer to this question clearly is in the affirmative. What the correlations in this table indicate is that high uniqueness scores and high output scores tend to go together even though measured from different samples of ideational behavior. Males and females again yielded similar results when analyzed separately. The individual with a high output of ideas when

TABLE 2.10

Correlations between Total Number of Ideas (N)
and Total Unique Ideas (U) for Noncontaminated Comparisons

	Uses-N	Pattern meanings-N	Similarities-N	Line meanings-N
Uses-U		.37	.54	.36
Pattern meanings-U	.55		.58	.63
Similarities-U	.48	.43		.36
Line meanings-U	.46	.66	.52	

Note — Data based on the 502 members of the sample for whom SAT scores were available.

dealing with the similarities task, for example, will tend to display a large number of unique ideas when he deals with the line meanings task. Analogously, someone with many unique ideational responses to the similarities procedure will tend to offer a large total output of ideas when responding to the line meanings task. The relationships depicted in Table 2.10 are free from any artifactual inflation because number and uniqueness measures are never correlated from the same task but always from different tasks. We can assume, therefore, that the magnitudes of the correlations shown in the table are fairly representative of the degree to which we can expect measures of ideational output and of number of unique ideas to correspond with one another. As would be predicted from the work that we noted in the preceding chapter, this degree is substantial. Recall that such a relationship can be readily accounted for on the ground that relatively common ideas are known to come earlier, and relatively unique ideas later, in a thought sequence that has been elicited by a task request of the kind used in our procedures — as, for example, to name uses for a particular object. The more ideas a person suggests, in other words, the more likely he is to suggest relatively unusual ones.

While the correlations shown in Table 2.10 are substantial, they are not, however, so high as to indicate that the output and uniqueness measures are fully equivalent. Room still exists for some divergence between the two. There will only be a certain degree of correspondence, in other words, between the orderings of individuals that would be obtained if we array them in terms of highest to lowest scores for total number of ideas and for number of unique ideas. To the extent that these orderings do differ, we may be able to determine whether number or uniqueness of ideas constitutes the more significant cognitive characteristic behind the display of talented nonacademic accomplishments. If criterion validation of this sort is to be obtained at all, we may discover that it does not apply in equal degree to the two ideational characteristics under study, but rather to one of them in particular. What we have found, then, is that the two characteristics are sufficiently different in terms of the orderings of individuals that will result from applying each of them as to render empirically feasible our goal of trying to treat them separately. We will want to keep number and uniqueness of ideas separated for purposes of comparison, therefore, in our further work.

As in the case of intelligence, equally weighted transformations of the scores that tapped a given ideational characteristic were summed to yield a single index. Since we expected our most reliable estimate of a person's ideational output to consist in his overall output on the four tasks that we have described, the distribution of total number of ideas was converted to standard score form in the case of each task. The four standard scores pertaining to each person's ideational productivity then were added together, yielding a single number reflecting our best estimate of how fluent he was in producing ideas. A comparable procedure was followed with regard to uniqueness of ideational content. For each task, the distribution of total number of unique ideas was transformed to standard scores. Each person's standard scores for number of unique ideas on the four tasks then were summed to provide a single best estimate of his productivity with respect to unique ideas in particular. The standard score transformations were based on the data for the entire sample. Obtained as a final result of these computations were two scores for each individual: one expressed his standing in the sample regarding number of ideas generated, while the other expressed his standing in the sample regarding the production of unique ideas. Each of these two scores was based upon giving equal weight to the person's performances on the four assessors to which he was exposed — uses, pattern meanings, similarities, and line meanings.

What, in absolute terms, were the number of ideas, and of unique ideas, produced on these various procedures? We already know from Table 2.3 that unique ideas comprise a relatively small proportion of the total ideational output. In order to obtain a more concrete impression of how the students dealt with the various tasks, however, it is useful to view the mean ideational output and mean number of unique ideas provided in response to each procedure. Table 2.11 presents these data for the sample as a whole and also — since the women tended to exceed the men on these indicators — for each sex separately. We note that the average person tended to offer something on the order of 20 ideas in thinking about the items comprising one of the tasks, and that about three of those ideas on the average turned out to be unique. But note in addition that the variability across individuals both as to the total number of ideas offered and also as to the number of unique ideas presented was considerable. Various students dealt with these tasks with wide individual differences. While the means for the uniqueness measures were considerably lower than those for the output measures so that distributional problems might have been encountered

TABLE 2.11

*Total Number of Ideas and Total Unique Ideas
by Task for the Members of the Sample*

	Entire sample (N = 502)		Men (N = 302)		Women (N = 200)	
	Mean	SD	Mean	SD	Mean	SD
Number of ideas						
Uses	28.07	16.81	26.38	15.81	30.61	17.96
Pattern meanings	15.63	10.98	14.48	10.42	17.37	11.60
Similarities	19.35	11.15	18.41	11.74	20.77	10.07
Line meanings	16.29	9.65	15.24	9.65	17.87	9.47
Uniqueness of ideas						
Uses	2.21	4.09	2.06	4.00	2.43	4.21
Pattern meanings	5.19	5.84	4.99	5.55	5.49	6.26
Similarities	1.02	1.94	1.02	2.21	1.01	1.44
Line meanings	2.96	3.99	2.65	3.68	3.41	4.40

Note — The N comprises all members of the sample for whom SAT scores were available.

with the former, no such problems seemed to arise. Rather, all correlational outcomes for the two kinds of measures were fully consistent.

One of the sources of these wide individual differences is of no moment to us — namely, the tendency for women to generate more ideas and more unique ideas than men. Recall that a similar situation arose in our finding that women obtained considerably higher verbal SAT scores than men. This sex bias favoring women on productivity and uniqueness of ideas as well as on verbal SAT scores apparently is not sufficient to produce much of a relationship between these ideational and intellective measures, however, or there would be more of a tendency than has been found for verbal SAT level to correlate with number and uniqueness of ideas. As we recall from Table 2.9, such correlation is minimal. Still, just as we did not want a higher intelligence group to contain disproportionately more women and fewer men than a lower intelligence group, so also we would not want a group higher in ideational productivity to contain a disproportionately greater number of women and smaller number of men than a group lower in ideational productivity, and similarly in the case of ideational uniqueness. As a consequence, we will want to define a student's ideational productivity level relative to the distribution for his sex when we compare in regard to other criteria persons who are higher and lower in their output of ideas. Thus, our higher ideational productivity group will consist of men who are high among the men and women who are high among the women in number of ideas produced, while our lower ideational productivity group will, in a comparable manner, consist of men who are low among the men and women who are low among the women in idea output. The analogous point applies for uniqueness of ideas. The plan just outlined eliminates any possible confounding of ideational productivity or uniqueness with the sex of the respondent. By proceeding in this fashion we will be able to test our theses in a manner which is nonspecific with regard to sex of respondent — the appropriate approach in light of the fact that our theses were not formulated in sex-specific terms. According to our formulation, in other words, men of higher and lower ideational productivity are expected to differ in the same way as women of higher and lower ideational productivity. So also, men of higher and lower ideational uniqueness are expected to differ in the same way as women of higher and lower ideational uniqueness. Armed with the findings that we have been considering on intelligence, number of ideas, and uniqueness of ideas, we are now in a position to form the groups of persons for evaluating the two theses of this book.

We have demonstrated that ideational output and uniqueness both are relatively distinct from intelligence but also are separable in some degree from each other. We have in hand, then, two cognitive characteristics either or both of which may further our understanding concerning who will display talented nonacademic accomplishments, if we in fact find — as we have predicted — that intelligence differences will not be of help in this regard. How, then, can we provide the most incisive test of our theses? Recall the methodological implications of Werts's (1967) critique of the Holland-Richards research, as discussed in the first chapter. Werts pointed out that correlation coefficients can be low when one of the variables concerns rare events such as talented nonacademic forms of accomplishments, even though such accomplishments still show a substantial relationship with some other type of information about the student — in Werts's case, academic achievement level. In order to demonstrate the relationship, Werts contrasted groups of high and low academic achievers and found them to differ accordingly in regard to the incidence of talented nonacademic accomplishments. Since we wish to demonstrate that these accomplishments show no relationship with intelligence, we must take account of the Werts critique by providing as sensitive a means as possible for the detection of such a relationship. Detectability should be maximized if we contrast groups that score relatively high and relatively low on intelligence. If extreme groups of this kind do not differ regarding talented forms of nonacademic accomplishments, then we will have a compelling basis for arguing against the role of intelligence in these matters — providing also that the high and low intelligence groups *do* differ in the expected direction regarding their academic achievements. But we want to do more than this. We also wish to show that a person's typical level of ideational productivity and/or uniqueness has the kind of positive relationship with talented nonacademic attainments that intelligence does not. This means demonstrating that when ideational output or uniqueness receives the same chance as intelligence to display itself as relevant

to nonacademic accomplishments, number and/or uniqueness of ideas — but not intelligence — is found to possess
this kind of relevance.

The requirements for proceeding with our work now
become clear. Equivalently extreme groups of students must
be formed in terms of each of three contrasts: students of
high and low intelligence, of high and low ideational productivity, and of high and low ideational uniqueness. If our
theses are fulfilled, talented forms of nonacademic accomplishment will be not at all associated with the first contrast,
but will be substantially associated with the second and/or
the third contrast. On the other hand, academic achievement
should be substantially related to the first contrast — thus
offering assurance that the intelligence range was not unduly
restricted. How extreme, in turn, should the groupings be?
There is, of course, no automatic way of answering this
question. We wanted the groups to be sufficiently extreme
that intelligence would receive every possible chance to display its potency — yet not so extreme as to reduce dras-
tically the number of people under study. Using upper and
lower thirds as our basis for defining groups seemed to
provide the most reasonable response to both considerations.
Recall also our requirement that such groupings be worked
out on a within-sex basis in order to avoid any confounding
with sex differences regarding the contrasts in question.
The high intelligence group refers, therefore, to those
students within the upper third of the intelligence score
distribution for the members of their sex, while the low
intelligence group refers to those students within the lower
third of the intelligence score distribution for the members of their sex. Analogous points apply for defining the
groups high and low in ideational productivity and the
groups high and low in ideational uniqueness. In each case,
the highs are those in the upper third of the score distribution
in question for the members of their sex; the lows, those
in the lower third of the appropriate within-sex score dis-

tribution. The divisions were made as near as possible to actual thirds as tied scores would allow.

Tables 2.12 through 2.14 present the sample sizes that result from forming the groups that are high and low on intelligence, ideational productivity, and ideational uniqueness, in the manner just described. The starting base for defining upper and lower thirds within sex on each of the three characteristics was provided by the 502 members of the sample (302 men, 200 women) for whom we possessed SAT scores. The group sizes that are shown in these tables are used in all of our subsequent analyses of the data, unless otherwise noted. While our hypotheses are expected to apply without regard to sex, so that the crucial test in every case is for the sexes combined, we will also present tests for the sexes considered separately so that the degree to which each sex conforms to the overall result can be directly observed. Our statistical evaluation of any comparison will consist quite simply of a t test between the high and low groups. As many writers have pointed out (see, for example, Boneau, 1960), the t test is a very "robust" statistical technique — that is, it is relatively impervious to the distributional characteristics of the scores undergoing analysis as long as the sample sizes are sufficiently large. As Tables 2.12 through 2.14 indicate, our samples are quite sizable in all cases.

A fitting way of closing this chapter is to cast our theses from the preceding chapter into the form of propositions that relate to the sample contrasts just described. Our testing framework is provided by the types of persons defined in Tables 2.12, 2.13, and 2.14. How, then, do our theses relate to the students in these tables? First, as our demonstration that the intelligence range of our sample is not subject to undue restriction, we hypothesize that high versus low intelligence in the Table 2.12 groups will be linked to a statistically significant degree with customary criteria of academic achievement. Such an outcome would validate the meaning of the intelligence contrast. We have, in turn, no

TABLE 2.12

Sample Sizes for the High and Low Intelligence Groups

	High intelligence	Low intelligence
Total	$N = 168$	$N = 170$
Men	$N = 101$	$N = 102$
Women	$N = 67$	$N = 68$

TABLE 2.13

Sample Sizes for the High and Low Ideational Productivity Groups

	High productivity	Low productivity
Total	$N = 167$	$N = 169$
Men	$N = 100$	$N = 101$
Women	$N = 67$	$N = 68$

TABLE 2.14

Sample Sizes for the High and Low Ideational Uniqueness Groups

	High uniqueness	Low uniqueness
Total	$N = 166$	$N = 167$
Men	$N = 100$	$N = 99$
Women	$N = 66$	$N = 68$

particular hypothesis about a linkage between ideational productivity level in the Table 2.13 groups and academic achievement, or between ideational uniqueness level in the Table 2.14 groups and academic achievement. Next, we expect that high versus low intelligence in the Table 2.12 groups will be unrelated to level of talented accomplishment in each of the various nonacademic domains under study —

that is, that there will be *no* significant linkage with intelligence for any of the analyses concerning nonacademic forms of talented attainments. Finally, we hypothesize that the kinds of talented attainments in question will show a statistically significant linkage with high versus low ideational output in the Table 2.13 groups, with high versus low ideational uniqueness in the Table 2.14 groups, or with both output and uniqueness. If this last hypothesis is sustained, furthermore, we can seek clues as to whether the productivity or the uniqueness aspect of a person's stream of ideas is the more important causal agent behind the linkage with nonacademic attainments by comparing the relative strengths of the effects found for the Table 2.13 groups and the Table 2.14 groups.

The next order of business is to demonstrate that the high versus low intelligence groups defined in our work represent an intelligence range that is sufficiently broad as to eventuate in substantial relationships between intelligence level and academic achievement. We turn to this matter in the chapter following.

Chapter 3

Achievement in the Classroom

If the distinction between high and low intelligence groups made in the last chapter is valid, we should find high and low intelligence students displaying quite different levels of academic achievement. Since the SAT is known to have a relationship with classroom achievement, such an outcome would come as no surprise per se. It would provide us, however, with assurance that the intelligence range represented by our sample bears the same kind of relationship with grade achievement as would be expected to hold for a more extreme intelligence contrast. The appropriate conclusion hence would be that the contrast between high and low intelligence groups in our investigation is a meaningful one in terms of the traditional connotations of the intelligence concept.

Two ways of probing the academic accomplishment levels of our students were utilized: examination of their academic performance in high school, and of their academic performance during the freshman year of college. We shall consider each in turn.

The student's academic achievement in high school was evaluated by assessing his class-rank position, expressed in relation to the size of his class. Class rank is a standard means utilized by high schools to report the academic standing of their seniors for purposes of college application. But how, more exactly, was this class-rank information used? To consider a student's academic rank in relation to the size of his class is to form a proportion, such as 1 over 130, or 2 over 15, or 38 over 45, the value of which is a smaller fraction as the rank is higher or the class size is larger. Class size must be considered in this manner, of course, since the meaning of a rank is not absolute but rather depends upon how many individuals have been ranked. To be fifth in a class of 10 obviously has a different meaning than to be fifth in a class of 250. Expressing the rank as a proportion of the number of students being ranked takes care of this problem.

Note the further problem, however, that a student with a high rank in a small class pushes up against what may be an unfair limit by which his academic record will be viewed. Take a student ranking 1 in a class of 5, compared with the student ranking 100 in a class of 500. Both end up with the same proportion — .20 — even though the former student has been categorized on the basis of much less precise information than the latter. In order to correct this tendency to penalize high ranking students from small classes, 0.5 is subtracted from each rank before the proportion is formed. Now the student who ranks 1 in a class of 5 receives .10 as the proportion expressing his relative rank, while the student who ranks 100 in a class of 500 still receives the proportion value of .20. The kind of adjusted proportion just described is arrived at by subtracting 0.5 from a student's rank in class and dividing by the size of his class. This adjusted proportion has been recommended by the makers of the SAT (College Entrance Examination Board, 1964) as a way of converting rank in high school class into a form that can be used for studying the relationship between SAT scores and high school academic achievement.

The adjusted proportion itself, in turn, must undergo a further conversion before we are through. It is necessary to take account of the fact that proportions around midway between 0 and 1 are much more frequently encountered — and hence tend to exert greater weight — than proportions near either extreme. To equalize the weight that different proportions will exert, therefore, the College Entrance Examination Board (1964) recommends a transformation of the adjusted proportions to a scale that gives greater weight to the extreme proportions than to those near the middle. The proportion values from 0 to 1 are transformed to a scale that runs from 80 to 20 — a change which also, by the way, results in smaller proportions (and hence higher levels of academic achievement) now being expressed by larger absolute numbers. This is a useful state of affairs since it involves less cognitive strain on the investigator's part to think of better academic performance in terms of larger numbers rather than in terms of smaller numbers. To indicate how this transformation is carried out, here follow the numerical values to which the indicated proportions are transformed: proportions from 0 to .001 become 80; from .002 to .005 become 77; from .006 to .011 become 74; from .012 to .025 become 71; from .026 to .049 become 68; from .050 to .088 become 65; from .089 to .146 become 62; from .147 to .226 become 59; from .227 to .325 become 56; from .326 to .439 become 53; from .440 to .560 become 50; from .561 to .674 become 47; from .675 to .773 become 44; from .774 to .853 become 41; from .854 to .911 become 38; from .912 to .950 become 35; from .951 to .974 become 32; from .975 to .988 become 29; from .989 to .994 become 26; from .995 to .998 become 23; and from .999 to 1 become 20. We now have an expression for a student's academic rank in his high school class as of the senior year such that the extreme of highest academic achievement is reflected in an assigned score of 80; medium academic achievement receives a score of 50; and the extreme of lowest academic achievement is reflected in an assigned score of 20. This is the scale that was used, then, for describing academic achievement in high school.

Table 3.1 compares the high and low intelligence groups in regard to high school academic achievement. A word first about the arrangement of information in this table, since the same arrangement will be followed in our subsequent analyses as well. Entered for the sexes combined and for each sex separately are the mean score values on the measure under examination. Beneath each mean, the standard deviation is shown in parentheses. The difference between the means in a given row is evaluated by the t entry for that row. Next to the t value is shown the statistical significance level that pertains to it for a two-tailed test, with information provided as to whether the obtained difference is not significant (n.s.), would occur less than 5 times in 100 by mere chance ($<.05$), would occur less than 2 times in 100 by mere chance ($<.02$), would occur less than 1 time in 100 by mere chance ($<.01$), or would occur less than 1 time in 1000 by mere chance ($<.001$). The major finding always is that shown in the first row — that is, for both sexes combined.

TABLE 3.1

Average Academic Achievement in High School
for the High and Low Intelligence Groups

	High intelligence	Low intelligence	t	p
Total	68.75 (5.93)	65.69 (6.70)	4.43	$<.001$
Men	67.64 (5.63)	65.29 (7.15)	2.60	$<.02$
Women	70.42 (6.03)	66.30 (5.96)	3.98	$<.001$

Note — One female member of the low intelligence group is missing, because she lacked high school achievement data.

From Table 3.1 we see that the high intelligence students earn substantially higher class ranks than their low intelligence counterparts. The overall relationship is significant beyond the .001 level. As far as academic performance in the high school years is concerned, then, it is evident that the high and low intelligence groups show the kind of achievement difference that we would expect if the intelligence difference between them is a meaningful one. Both groups are above average in high school academic performance, to be sure, but the high intelligence subjects still earn consistently higher grades than the low intelligence subjects. For the intelligence range represented by our sample as well as for a broader intelligence spread, therefore, higher intelligence is associated with superior academic performance in high school.

When we turn to Tables 3.2 and 3.3, we find a serendipitous outcome that had not been particularly predicted. It is that ideational productivity — and to a lesser extent, ideational uniqueness — seem to exert significant effects on high school academic performance. Since high or low status on ideational productivity or uniqueness is virtually independent of high or low status on intelligence, ideational flow on the one hand and intelligence on the other are making relatively separate contributions to a student's high school grade level. But productivity and uniqueness of ideas seem, furthermore, to be differentiated in regard to their contributions to academic performance. Comparing Tables 3.2 and 3.3 suggests that productivity counts for more than uniqueness in this regard. If productivity with respect to ideas does in fact reflect a person's typical level of cognitive energy or ideational activation, then its strong linkage with high school academic achievement in Table 3.2 would seem to make sense. It is understandable that those students with a stronger disposition to generate ideas might engage in a more extensive range or depth of work in connection with any academic course. Greater coverage of this kind —

TABLE 3.2

Average Academic Achievement in High School
for the High and Low Ideational Productivity Groups

	High productivity	Low productivity	t	p
Total	68.41	65.18	4.43	<.001
	(6.07)	(7.21)		
Men	67.67	63.72	3.96	<.001
	(6.25)	(7.80)		
Women	69.52	67.41	2.17	<.05
	(5.66)	(5.55)		

Note — Two female members of the low productivity group are missing, because they lacked high school achievement data.

TABLE 3.3

Average Academic Achievement in High School
for the High and Low Ideational Uniqueness Groups

	High uniqueness	Low uniqueness	t	p
Total	67.33	65.55	2.40	<.02
	(6.23)	(7.30)		
Men	66.38	64.30	2.07	<.05
	(6.27)	(7.83)		
Women	68.77	67.41	1.31	n.s.
	(5.91)	(6.01)		

Note — Two female members of the low uniqueness group are missing because they lacked high school achievement data.

delving into more of the nooks and crannies connected with a given subject — might well eventuate in a higher grade. Since, of course, productivity and uniqueness are related, the strong linkage of the former with high school grades is sufficient to account also for the weak linkage displayed by the latter with high school grades. There is no need to assume, in other words, that more than productivity is operating here.

At the least, then, intelligence relates to high school academic performance in a manner that validates the customary meaning of the intelligence indicator as holding for the range defined by our sample. In addition, ideational productivity may make a contribution to such academic performance as well. The results on all these matters were quite analogous when examined separately for the members of each sex. We turn next to the comparable kinds of questions regarding academic performance during the freshman year of college.

Colleges are in the habit of computing a simple indicator of a student's overall academic achievement — the quality point ratio. This is an average which takes account of the fact that some college courses earn a student more credit hours than others, and weights the student's grade in accordance with the number of credit hours that pertain to the course in question. Thus, for example, a chemistry course may earn the student four credit hours; a history tutorial, two. The grade earned in the former course hence will count twice as heavily in the quality point ratio as will the grade earned in the latter. To arrive at a student's quality point ratio for the freshman year, we used the following standard scale of numerical equivalences for his letter grades: a grade of A was called 4, B was called 3, C was called 2, D was called 1, and F or failure was called 0. The number equivalent for the grade achieved in each course was multiplied by the number of credit hours for the course, yielding what are called quality points. The sum of the quality points earned was divided by the number of credit hours attempted, providing an index that ranges from 0 to 4 and expresses the student's mean grade achievement level per credit hour. We worked from each student's grade transcript for the freshman year, including in our computations the grades earned in all courses of an academic nature. Thus, for example, grades for swimming or for wrestling were not included. A quality point ratio of 2, then, would represent an average letter grade of C, while a quality point ratio of 4 would represent a straight A record.

Tables 3.4, 3.5, and 3.6 present for the freshman year quality point ratios the same kind of information as was contained in Tables 3.1 through 3.3 for academic achievement in high school. The results turn out to be quite comparable. Consider Table 3.4 first. Contrasted here are the groups high and low on intelligence. Once again we find a strong intelligence effect: the high intelligence students earn higher quality point ratios than do the low intelligence students. On Table 3.5 we also find replicated for first year college grades the unexpected outcome that we noted on Table 3.2 for high school grades: the high ideational productivity group earns higher grades than the group low on ideational productivity. The mean difference in freshman college grades is greater, however, when we compare high and low

TABLE 3.4

Freshman Quality Point Ratio
for the High and Low Intelligence Groups

	High intelligence	Low intelligence	t	p
Total	2.74 (0.63)	2.24 (0.60)	7.46	< .001
Men	2.62 (0.66)	2.21 (0.63)	4.51	< .001
Women	2.92 (0.53)	2.28 (0.55)	6.79	< .001

TABLE 3.5

Freshman Quality Point Ratio
for the High and Low Ideational Productivity Groups

	High productivity	Low productivity	t	p
Total	2.59 (0.68)	2.38 (0.67)	2.88	<.01
Men	2.54 (0.76)	2.26 (0.70)	2.65	<.01
Women	2.68 (0.55)	2.55 (0.60)	1.26	n.s.

Note — One male member of the high productivity group is missing because he lacked freshman college grade data.

TABLE 3.6

Freshman Quality Point Ratio for the High
and Low Ideational Uniqueness Groups

	High uniqueness	Low uniqueness	t	p
Total	2.53 (0.66)	2.42 (0.66)	1.46	n.s.
Men	2.45 (0.72)	2.35 (0.70)	0.97	n.s.
Women	2.65 (0.54)	2.53 (0.59)	1.23	n.s.

Note — One male member of the high uniqueness group is missing because he lacked freshman college grade data.

intelligence groups than it is when comparing high and low ideational productivity groups. Turning to Table 3.6, where the groups high and low on ideational uniqueness are contrasted, we find no linkage between ideational uniqueness and grades in college. The lack of a relationship between uniqueness and grades makes clear that the ideational productivity contrast is solely responsible for the link with first year college grades, rather than sharing its contribution with uniqueness. Similar pictures are again found for the sexes considered separately, except that the link between ideational productivity and college grades exists mainly among males.

Level of academic achievement in college as well as in high school, therefore, provides clear validating evidence for the distinction between high and low intelligence groups in our sample. High intelligence is linked with the achievement of higher grades. Moreover, ideational productivity seems also to make a contribution to grade level in college as it did in high school. This effect, furthermore, is not shared with uniqueness of ideas but rather is specific to number of ideas produced. It is as if the student who generates a larger output of ideas on a topic will tend to do so in connection with academic course material as well, with the consequence that he digs somewhat more thoroughly into the content of the course. But the major empirical message in the present findings is that our hypothesized link between intelligence and average academic accomplishment in college receives very strong confirmation.

We have been able to demonstrate, then, the basic point at which this chapter was aimed. There is no doubt that high versus low intelligence as defined in our sample carries the same general kind of validity in terms of academic achievement criteria as would a more extensive spread regarding intelligence levels. The intelligence contrast which our sample provides is quite sufficient to generate the customary connections between higher intelligence and superior academic performance. We can be quite clear, therefore, about what high versus low levels of intelligence mean in our sample — they mean differences in grade-getting ability. Armed with this knowledge, we can proceed to ask what these intelligence differences do *not* mean.

Chapter 4

Talented
Accomplishments
outside the Classroom

To obtain information about talented accomplishments that took place outside of the requirements placed upon the student by academic work, the entering freshmen in our study were asked to look back over their high school years. Various questions were aimed at assessing what the student had been doing during the last four years in regard to each of a number of domains of potential extracurricular involvement. The choice of domains on our part was dictated by the aim of including all areas wherein forms of nonacademic excellence might be displayed that would primarily reflect aesthetic, scientific, or social skills. A further requirement was that the areas be accessible to members of both sexes, so that it would be reasonable to expect the results to replicate across the sexes. Excluded from consideration, for example, was athletic prowess, for which physical agility would constitute a major factor; involvement in extracurricular jobs, for which economic need would constitute an important determinant and for which entrepreneurial connotations would be more likely in the case of males; and concern with the dance as an art form, for which access would be essentially restricted to females.

The materials, which drew heavily upon the work of the Holland-Richards group cited in Chapter 1, concerned the following areas: exercise of leadership in student organizations, attainments in the visual arts, commitment to social service activities, accomplishments in the field of writing, achievements in the dramatic arts, attainments in music, and involvement in forms of scientific work. Administered as part of what was mailed to the incoming freshmen during the summer after their acceptance and prior to their arrival on campus, the questions were preceded by the general introduction described at the beginning of Chapter 2. It was clear to the students, then, that responding was fully optional on their part, with nothing of an academic nature contingent upon whether or how they replied. Thus, they were looking back upon the last four years of their lives at a point in time when they were secure in the knowledge of their acceptance at college, and they also had received our assurances that their participation in answering these questions was completely voluntary.

The following statement served as a preface for the task:

> Listed below are items describing some possible achievements of students. If an item is descriptive of you, please place an X in the space provided. Do not include achievements or activities occurring before the ninth grade.

The statements which the students were asked to consider as possibly descriptive of themselves were grouped according to the seven areas noted before — leadership, art, social service, writing, drama, music, and science. Each area was named above the statements that pertained to it. The number of items for each area varied between three and six,

depending simply on the number of statements that seemed
natural for covering a student's potential attainments in the
area in question. Debating was grouped with dramatic arts
because of its emphasis on histrionic ability in the making of
effective speeches. The areas and items were arranged in
the sequence that follows, which duplicates the protocol seen
by each student, except that the students' version contained
a line in front of each item for marking an X and did not
contain any letter designations for the items:

LEADERSHIP

a. Participated as an active member of one or more student
organizations
b. Nominated for or appointed to office in a student organization
c. Elected president or chairman of a student organization
d. Elected president of student government or class

ART

a. Created art work such as painting, drawing, sculpturing,
cartooning, photography (not as part of a course)
b. Had art work exhibited or published
c. Entered an artistic competition or contest
d. Won a prize or an award in art competition

SOCIAL SERVICE

a. Actively participated in programs sponsored by community or religious group, such as Scouts, 4-H Clubs,
YMCA, YWCA, YMHA, CYO
b. Elected or appointed officer of such a group
c. Received an award or prize for work in service group

LITERATURE

a. Wrote original poems, plays, stories, articles, essays (not
as part of a course), but have not published

b. Published original writings in school paper
c. Had original writings published in public newspaper, magazine, anthology (not school publication)
d. Won a literary prize for creative writing
e. Worked on editorial staff of school paper or annual
f. Edited school paper or annual

DRAMATIC ARTS

a. Participated in activities of speech, debate or dramatic group
b. Played minor role in cast or crew of plays sponsored by school, community, or religious groups; or entered debate or speech contest
c. Played major role in dramatic production
d. Received an award for acting, playwriting, or other phase of dramatic production
e. Won an award in a state or regional speech or debate contest

MUSIC

a. Played a musical instrument
b. Sang as a soloist or member of a group
c. Composed or arranged music
d. Performed music with school or community group
e. Won prize or award in musical competition
f. Participation as a regular professional musician, or had professional performance given of music composed or arranged

SCIENCE

a. Participated as a member of a science club or reading and discussion group
b. Built a piece of equipment or laboratory apparatus (not as a part of a course)

c. Appointed teaching or laboratory assistant

d. Entered a scientific competition

e. Won first, second, or third prize in a state or regional science contest

f. Attended a summer science program sponsored by the National Science Foundation

It is clear from what was said before that nothing of an extrinsic kind depended on the students' replies to these queries, and we have every reason to assume that the students believed this. Still, is there any further evidence that can be offered to document the view that their replies were reasonably undistorted and veridical? If the descriptions are veridical, they should be discriminating — that is, more students should endorse some items than others, depending on whether the items are describing accomplishments that are more frequently encountered or more rare. It is rather easy, as a matter of fact, to state for every item in the foregoing materials whether we would expect few or many students to exhibit the attainment in question. How well will these expectations be matched by the actual frequencies of endorsement that were obtained? If the match is a good one, it seems fair to conclude that veridicality of self-descriptions most likely was high. If, on the other hand, we encountered blanket endorsements that displayed minimal differences between those attainments that we would expect to be relatively common and those which should occur only infrequently, then the data would be suspect.

Table 4.1 permits us to examine this matter for all three kinds of groups — those high and low on intelligence, on ideational output, and on uniqueness of ideas. Comparison of the obtained percentages of endorsement with the content of the respective items indicates quite clearly that the students were indeed making the kinds of discriminations that veridicality would lead us to expect. Consider some examples. In the area of leadership, practically everyone indicated that

TABLE 4.1

Percentage of Endorsement for Each Self-Descriptive Item

Item	High and low intelligence groups ($N = 338$)	High and low productivity groups ($N = 336$)	High and low uniqueness groups ($N = 333$)
Leadership			
(a)	93	95	95
(b)	83	85	83
(c)	50	48	49
(d)	12	15	14
Art			
(a)	34	34	33
(b)	11	12	12
(c)	6	9	8
(d)	4	5	4
Social Service			
(a)	73*	75*	74
(b)	45*	48*	47
(c)	21*	22*	22
Writing			
(a)	36*	40*	39
(b)	33*	37*	32
(c)	10*	10*	8
(d)	9*	10*	10
(e)	42*	43*	41
(f)	17*	19*	17

they had participated as active members of one or more student organizations (item *a*), but only a small proportion of the students reported that they had been elected president of their student government or high school class (item *d*). Or in the area of art, while about one-third of the students said

TABLE 4.1 (continued)

Percentage of Endorsement for Each Self-Descriptive Item

Item	High and low intelligence groups ($N = 338$)	High and low productivity groups ($N = 336$)	High and low uniqueness groups ($N = 333$)
Drama			
(a)	45*	50*	49
(b)	54*	56*	55
(c)	23*	22*	23
(d)	5*	6*	6
(e)	8*	10*	8
Music			
(a)	54	55	54
(b)	37	39	39
(c)	9	9	9
(d)	48	45	44
(e)	13	14	13
(f)	4	5	4
Science			
(a)	33	34	34
(b)	20	17	18
(c)	14	16	15
(d)	31	31	30
(e)	8	5	6
(f)	10	9	7

*These percentages are based on one less than the stated *N* for the respective columns because the booklet of one student who appears in both columns had been sent out lacking the relevant sheet.

they had created art work (item *a*), a much smaller percentage indicated that they had won a prize or an award in an art competition (item *d*). Regarding the dramatic arts, about half of the students reported that they had participated in the activities of a group concerned with speech, debating, or dramatics (item *a*), but very few described themselves as having received an award for acting, playwriting, or some other aspect of dramatic production (item *d*). To mention just one more domain, over half of the students reported that they played a musical instrument (item *a*), while only a few reported that they had composed or arranged music (item *c*). In like manner, the proportions of endorsements found for the various other items under consideration are consistent with how frequently we would expect the activities in question to be engaged in during the high school years. These proportions vary across a range extending from 5, 10, or 15 percent for accomplishments that should be relatively rare, to 50 percent or more for accomplishments that should be quite frequent. The various domains as such, furthermore, show expectable differences from one another regarding incidence of student accomplishments. Thus, for example, work in the visual arts is found rather rarely, while activities of a social service nature are undertaken more frequently. There seems to be a good basis for believing, then, that the self-descriptions provided about the kinds of talented non-academic accomplishments here surveyed are reasonably accurate.

How are the attainments that are depicted by the various items within a given domain related to one another? We already have noted that, within any domain, some of the items reflect attainments of a rarer kind than others — both in terms of the nature of the items and also in terms of the obtained empirical outcomes. The attainments are so described, furthermore, that a student who is able to report that a rare one applies to himself also is likely to be able to report or may even be required by logic to report that a more commonly encountered one within the same domain also applies to himself. The smaller percentages recorded within a given domain on Table 4.1, then, will tend to define a set of persons who also are included in the larger percentages.

As examples where the relationship between a more rare and a more common attainment is logically required, consider the following. The student who reports that he was elected president or chairman of a student organization — item (c) under the leadership category — also has to report that he was nominated for or appointed to an office in a student organization — item (b). To be elected, he must have been nominated first. A student who indicates that he won a prize in an art competition — item (d) under art — also must indicate that he has created art work — item (a). To win a prize for an art product, he must have created something of this kind. As another example of a necessary connection, the student who, in the area of science, reports that he won first, second, or third prize in a state or regional science contest (item e) also must indicate that he entered a scientific competition — item (d). If he had not entered, he could not have won. In other cases, however, the relationship between a more rare and a more common attainment is not a necessary one but only likely. Here are some examples. The student who has played a major role in a dramatic production — item (c) under dramatic arts — also is likely to have played minor roles in such productions — item (b). The student who has published original writings in a public newspaper, magazine, or anthology — item (c) under literature — also is likely to have written original poems, plays, stories, articles, or essays that have not been published — item (a). Or as a final example of a link that is likely but not necessary, a student who has won a prize in a state or regional science contest — item (e) under science — also is likely to have built a piece of equipment or laboratory apparatus — item (b).

Since it is unlikely or impossible, depending upon the case, to endorse relatively rare attainments within a given domain without also endorsing relatively common ones, summing the number of items endorsed by a student for a particular domain will give us an approximation to a quality index — a measure of the extent of his accomplishments in that domain, or how deeply he has penetrated it. Endorsing more items represents a higher level of attainment in a given area than endorsing fewer items; while endorsing one item represents a higher attainment level in that area than endorsing none at all. Before we turn to an examination of how degree of accomplishment in each domain taken separately is related to the intelligence level and ideational characteristics of the students, however, there is a broader question that we can ask of the data first.

Degree of penetration of a single domain tells us about the specialist; the person who has achieved high competence in one area of involvement. But what about the generalist? We refer here to what might be called the ideal of the Renaissance man — more fashionable in an earlier age than today, perhaps, but no less relevant. Who are the students exhibiting at least moderate competence at many things, as well as possibly very high competence at one or two kinds of pursuits among the many? Suppose we ask about breadth of accomplishments, in other words, while still remaining at least partially mindful of quality of accomplishment within any given area. Paying some attention both to breadth and depth of attainments should constitute a reasonable approximation to what the Renaissance ideal embodies.

How does one pay attention both to breadth and depth of talented nonacademic attainments? By considering not only the student's degree of attainment in a given area but also the number of areas with which he has concerned himself. Such a basis of reckoning disregards which areas are at issue in any given instance. Thus, suppose that we find one student with considerable accomplishments in writing, dramatics, and social service, and another who displays considerable attainments in art, music, and science. Both would earn comparably higher scores than a student with substantial attainments in leadership and music, say, or one displaying considerable prowess at science and art. The two latter students, in turn, would earn comparably higher scores than a student with high attainments in only one domain of involvement. So also, the student with moderately high attainments in many areas could earn as high a score as the student with stronger attainments in fewer areas. Since breadth and depth both count by the present set of standards, more of one can compensate for less of the other. While the extreme dilettante, on the other hand, can do moderately well in these terms by virtue of his breadth of coverage of many domains, he is limited to a particular ceiling upon the amount of credit that he can earn unless he also pursues one or more of these areas in greater depth. It is the true generalist, then, who receives the maximum reward by the present criteria, although the dilettante who spreads himself thinly may come out as well as someone who goes deeply into one area but disregards all the rest. Next we must consider how this aim of revealing the generalists among our students can be translated into practice.

Recall the listing presented earlier of our queries into the seven domains of potential nonacademic accomplishment under study. We noted that the number of statements representing each area varied between three and six. No domain, therefore, was represented by less than three items. In order to seek out the generalists, we want to give equal weight to accomplishments in each of the seven domains. It would do us no good, in other words, to give attainments in one domain more weight than those in another simply because more items were included about the former than the latter. Literature with its six items, for example, should not receive more emphasis than social service with its three items. Given variation in the number of queries aimed at each domain, however, how can equal weighting be achieved? By distinguishing within each domain among the following kinds of persons: those endorsing no items at all, those endorsing one, those endorsing two, and those endorsing three or more. A student's score within each of the seven domains represented in our inquiries hence has to range between 0 and 3, with the consequence that all domains play an equal role as potential contributors to the student's standing as a generalist. Once the student's score for each domain has been expressed in terms of the range of 0 to 3 as just described, all we need do is add the results together for all seven domains. We now have, in the case of any student, a single number that can range from 0 to 21. Each of the seven nonacademic domains under investigation has received an equal chance to contribute to this number. At the high extreme stands the person with strong attainments in all of the domains. At the opposite extreme, we find the person with no attainments in any of the areas. The higher the score earned by a person, the greater must be both the breadth of attainments across domains and the depth of attainment in each, since any one domain can contribute no more than three credits toward the theoretical maximum of 21.

The measure just described, then, tells us about the generality of a student's nonacademic accomplishments regardless of the particular domains at issue — in a word, to what extent the student is a generalist. How does generality of nonacademic accomplishments relate to intelligence level, ideational productivity, and ideational uniqueness? The findings are contained in Tables 4.2, 4.3, and 4.4, respectively.

Consider first the students high and low on intelligence. Table 4.2 presents the results. They confirm to an impressive degree our hypothesis that intelligence would have no bearing upon such accomplishments. It is quite apparent from Table 4.2 that the intelligence contrast exerts no effect at all upon generality of nonacademic accomplishments. Despite the use of a mode of analysis which takes account of Werts's proposals as to how one should seek to detect such effects, absolutely none is found. Turning to Table 4.3, we find that the number of ideas typically produced by the stu-

TABLE 4.2

*Generality of Nonacademic Accomplishments
for the High and Low Intelligence Groups*

	High intelligence	Low intelligence	t	p
Total	9.27 (3.91)	9.43 (4.10)	0.36	n.s.
Men	8.69 (3.84)	9.12 (4.32)	0.74	n.s.
Women	10.13 (3.86)	9.88 (3.73)	0.39	n.s.

Note — One male member of the low intelligence group is missing because he lacked the opportunity to report on certain types of accomplishments.

TABLE 4.3

*Generality of Nonacademic Accomplishments
for the High and Low Ideational Productivity Groups*

	High productivity	Low productivity	t	p
Total	10.66 (3.80)	8.71 (3.69)	4.77	< .001
Men	10.12 (3.93)	8.26 (3.78)	3.42	< .001
Women	11.46 (3.46)	9.38 (3.47)	3.49	< .001

Note — One male member of the high productivity group is missing because he lacked the opportunity to report on certain types of accomplishments.

TABLE 4.4

Generality of Nonacademic Accomplishments
for the High and Low Ideational Uniqueness Groups

	High uniqueness	Low uniqueness	t	p
Total	10.25 (4.00)	8.73 (3.76)	3.56	$<.001$
Men	9.59 (4.08)	8.62 (3.96)	1.71	n.s.
Women	11.24 (3.70)	8.90 (3.46)	3.79	$<.001$

dent, on the other hand, exerts a pervasive impact upon generality of nonacademic accomplishments. Our hypothesis to this effect hence also receives strong confirmation. The contrast is significant well beyond the .001 level for both sexes combined, and even beyond the .001 level for each sex considered separately. The student with high ideational output shows greater generality of nonacademic accomplishments than the student with low ideational output. With the effect from high versus low output of ideas significant beyond the .001 level and the effect from high versus low intelligence levels nil, the contrast between the two is very clear indeed as far as their respective implications for nonacademic accomplishments are concerned. What about uniqueness of ideas? From Table 4.4 we find that high versus low uniqueness also exerts a strong effect upon generality of nonacademic accomplishments. The two sexes yielded analogous patterns of results in regard to all of these findings, except that the uniqueness contrast showed up less well than the ideational productivity contrast for the males.

While the overall effect generated by uniqueness of ideas is quite sizable, we note in comparing Tables 4.3 and 4.4 that the parallel overall effect produced by ideational productivity is larger still: in the first rows of the respective tables we find a t of 4.77 for high versus low productivity groups and a t of 3.56 for high versus low uniqueness groups. We are led to suspect, therefore, that output of ideas per se, rather than uniqueness of ideas in particular, is the more potent influence upon the generality of a student's nonacademic accomplishments.

Our inquiry into the generality issue thus has yielded clear results. The students who produce larger numbers of ideas also tend to be generalists in their talented accomplishments outside the academic curriculum. They show a wider variety of nonacademic attainments, while still displaying at least some depth along with this breadth. The same can be said, although to a somewhat lesser degree, of the students who produce larger numbers of unique ideas in particular. With ideational output as such exhibiting the more powerful linkage, however, a person's characteristic level of ideational activity — his cognitive energy level, if you will — may well be the crux of the matter as far as the present kind of generality is concerned. Since unique ideas are more likely to occur as larger numbers of ideas are generated, the present results would be expected if number of ideas — and hence whatever process is responsible for the generating of a larger output of ideas — were the governing consideration. Intelligence level, on the other hand, plays no role at all in regard to generality of nonacademic accomplishments. The high and the low intelligence students are quite similar as far as such generality is concerned.

But if the students with many ideas are found to be generalists when it comes to the world outside the classroom, will they also be found to penetrate a given domain of nonacademic accomplishment with much depth? From the way in which generality was defined, we know that this must be true to at least a limited degree: we were talking about an amalgam of breadth with depth, not about sheer dilettantism. Nevertheless, it is clear that the preceding approach to nonacademic accomplishments does not give the specialist his due, and it is possible that the specialist and the generalist in nonacademic pursuits are very different kinds of persons. It could be argued, then, that while level of ideational output is related to being a generalist and intelligence is unrelated to being a generalist, the situation becomes very different when we look at depth or quality of accomplishment in any particular nonacademic domain. It could be proposed that, as soon as we are talking about level of accomplishment within a given nonacademic domain, intelligence becomes more important and sheer fluency of ideas becomes less important. Such a proposal would run counter, of course, to our hypotheses. Is it borne out by the evidence?

We turn next to degree of accomplishment within each nonacademic domain considered separately. The measure in the case of any domain simply is the number of items endorsed. Its range hence depends upon the number of items that represent the domain in question. In studying depth of attainment within each domain, we shall take them up in the order in which they appeared in the listing presented earlier. The exercise of leadership in student organizations will be considered first.

Leadership, it will be recalled, was assessed from such events as election to the presidency of one's student government or high school class, election to the chairmanship or presidency of a student organization, and nomination for or appointment to office in a student organization. With four statements pertaining to leadership, a student's score could range from zero if none of the statements applied to him, up to a theoretical maximum of four if all of the statements applied to him. At issue in the present domain of nonacademic accomplishment is the extent to which the student came to exercise leadership functions in his dealings with his fellows in one or another kind of student organization.

Are high intelligence students more likely to be leaders than low intelligence students? The answer from the intelligence results presented in Table 4.5 clearly is no. Level of intelligence is unrelated to the exercise of leadership in student organizations. If anything, as a matter of fact, the direction of the leadership contrast is toward higher scores on leadership for the low intelligence students rather than for the high intelligence students. But the clear finding is an absence of any significant relationship between intelligence level and the exercise of leadership. The disposition to generate larger numbers of ideas, on the other hand, has a distinct positive bearing upon such leadership. We note in Table 4.6 that ideational productivity exerts an overall effect significant beyond the .001 level on leadership attainments, the high productivity group earning higher leadership scores than the lows. From Table 4.7 we also note, however, that the production of unique ideas as such has no significant bearing upon leadership. It is greater ideational output in general, therefore, not the tendency to produce unique ideas in particular, that is linked with higher attainments as a leader. All the findings just described were analogous for each sex considered separately.

TABLE 4.5

*Leadership Accomplishments
for the High and Low Intelligence Groups*

	High intelligence	Low intelligence	t	p
Total	2.30 (1.02)	2.45 (0.98)	1.43	n.s.
Men	2.29 (1.10)	2.44 (1.08)	1.01	n.s.
Women	2.31 (0.89)	2.47 (0.82)	1.07	n.s.

TABLE 4.6

*Leadership Accomplishments for the High and Low
Ideational Productivity Groups*

	High productivity	Low productivity	t	p
Total	2.63 (0.82)	2.24 (1.00)	3.93	$<.001$
Men	2.65 (0.93)	2.25 (1.03)	2.91	$<.01$
Women	2.60 (0.63)	2.22 (0.96)	2.69	$<.01$

TABLE 4.7

*Leadership Accomplishments for the High and Low
Ideational Uniqueness Groups*

	High uniqueness	Low uniqueness	t	p
Total	2.48 (0.90)	2.32 (1.01)	1.57	n.s.
Men	2.49 (1.01)	2.37 (1.05)	0.80	n.s.
Women	2.47 (0.71)	2.24 (0.95)	1.62	n.s.

The leadership domain, then, yields results suggesting
that having many ideas counts in a way that higher intelligence does not. The ability to come up with a more extensive
outpouring of ideational content seems to have a specific
bearing upon the exercise of leadership in student organizations — not just a general bearing upon extracurricular

attainments as a whole. It could be argued, however, that leadership calls for a kind of boisterous energy — in contrast to a fine-grained use of intellect — that makes understandable the link with ideational output and the absence of any connection with level of intelligence. Such an argument would imply that a line of nonacademic endeavor which is less characterized by boisterousness and bustle would not yield the same kind of results. A good contrast in this regard is provided by art — the domain to which we turn next. However else they differ, work in visual aesthetics implies less surface hecticness than the life of a successful student politician.

Potential attainments in the visual arts were explored by inquiring whether the student had created art work of one kind or another — such as painting, drawing, or sculpture; had exhibited or published such work; had entered such work in an artistic competition; and had won an award or prize as a result of such a competition. Level of accomplishment at any type of artistic endeavor concerning the visual modality hence was under consideration. What are the results? We find from Table 4.8 that intelligence status does not significantly

TABLE 4.8

Art Attainments for the High and Low Intelligence Groups

	High intelligence	Low intelligence	t	p
Total	0.49 (0.89)	0.60 (0.97)	1.11	n.s.
Men	0.37 (0.78)	0.53 (0.97)	1.32	n.s.
Women	0.67 (1.01)	0.71 (0.96)	0.20	n.s.

influence a student's attainments in the visual arts. If anything, as a matter of fact, the direction of the means — as we also noted regarding intelligence and leadership — is toward an association between higher intelligence status and lower rather than higher artistic attainments. Intelligence quite evidently does not contribute to competence in art. The clearest inference we can make is that intelligence has no effect in this domain.

When we turn to the productivity or uniqueness of the student's ideas, by contrast, a strikingly different picture emerges. Generating larger numbers of ideas is, as we see on Table 4.9, strongly linked with attainments in art: the overall effect is significant beyond the .001 level. From Table 4.10 we note that the same is true for the production of unique ideas in particular. Both aspects of a person's flow of ideas, then, display a positive relationship with art attainments. With the productivity and uniqueness overall effects both significant beyond the .001 level and the two t values quite similar (3.80 and 3.75, respectively), it is evident that counting unique ideas in particular does not provide any greater degree of leverage over predicting art attainments than is

TABLE 4.9

*Art Attainments for the High and Low
Ideational Productivity Groups*

	High productivity	Low productivity	t	p
Total	0.80 (1.16)	0.38 (0.79)	3.80	<.001
Men	0.66 (1.08)	0.28 (0.75)	2.91	<.01
Women	1.00 (1.24)	0.54 (0.84)	2.50	<.02

TABLE 4.10

*Art Attainments for the High and Low
Ideational Uniqueness Groups*

	High uniqueness	Low uniqueness	t	p
Total	0.77 (1.10)	0.38 (0.79)	3.75	< .001
Men	0.64 (1.04)	0.29 (0.73)	2.72	< .01
Women	0.97 (1.18)	0.50 (0.86)	2.65	< .01

afforded simply by knowing who produces more ideas in general. Having more ideas — and having more ideas that are unique — are characteristics that help define the artists in our sample. Intelligence is of no help at all in this regard. Once again, the various findings that we have described are quite comparable when each sex is considered separately.

Even though leadership in student organizations and work in the visual arts represent very different behavioral arenas, therefore, we begin to glimpse the possibility of a common cognitive thread running through both types of excellence — namely, a more ready flow of ideas. Could it be that success as a leader in student political activities and artistic attainments both call upon ideational resourcefulness on the individual's part — the generating of ideational possibilities which then can be applied to the needs of a given situation? Resourcefulness in coming up with ideas begins to look like a quite generic type of thinking capacity possessing relevance for a variety of life tasks — including ones for which greater intelligence seems to be of no help at all. We have more evidence to consider, however, and should not let our interpretations outpace our data. A critic still might want to propose at this point that work in the visual arts as well as leadership in student organizations happen to define forms of nonacademic accomplishments both of which fall outside the ken of intelligence as traditionally conceived: the latter, because it calls for a kind of extroverted boisterousness; the former, because it depends upon a quite specialized set of visual sensitivities that may reflect themselves in greater image-making skills and hence a more ready flow of ideas for that reason. The critic would go on to argue that nonacademic accomplishment domains that make heavy demands upon verbal or mathematical skills, on the other hand, will display a linkage with intelligence. Thus, for example, he would claim that the more intelligent students will excel at creative writing because of the prominent place of verbal ability in the concept of intelligence, and that the more intelligent students will excel at scientific endeavors outside the classroom because mathematical ability also is of central importance to the intelligence concept. These potential criticisms will be confronted directly when we consider the results for nonacademic attainments in writing and in science.

Commitment to social service activities is the domain that was listed next for the students. The difference between this category and leadership in student organizations is that here we are primarily concerned with groups that emphasize service to others, while the leadership category emphasizes political ascendancy over one's peers. In the case of social service groups, at issue is the disposition to devote effort toward pursuing humanitarian functions in relation to one's fellow man: helping out in neighborhood centers for underprivileged youths, serving as a counselor in a settlement house camp that gets children of economically deprived families off the city streets and into the country for a few weeks during the summer, providing remedial tutoring in the hope of putting minority group children with insufficient prior schooling on their academic feet when they are injected into a better school, bringing news and demonstrations of agricultural aids and technical advances to rural farmers who wouldn't otherwise hear of them. An abiding concern with ethical or religious values, in other words, tends to be reflected in these activities. How do the groups under study compare regarding social service commitments?

Table 4.11 indicates that intelligence once again is unrelated to the domain in question. For the females alone in this table, there is a nonsignificant trend toward a linkage. With the trend falling short of significance, however, the most appropriate conclusion to draw is that intelligence and social service commitments show no clear relationship. The same conclusion is indicated by the results in Tables 4.12 and 4.13 for ideational productivity and uniqueness, respectively. Here again, no significant effects are obtained in any comparison made — whether overall or for either sex separately. Intelligence level, ideational output, and ideational uniqueness, all are found to be without any clear bearing, therefore, upon the social service commitments

TABLE 4.11

Social Service Commitments
for the High and Low Intelligence Groups

	High intelligence	Low intelligence	t	p
Total	1.46 (1.06)	1.33 (1.04)	1.21	n.s.
Men	1.32 (1.06)	1.31 (1.07)	0.07	n.s.
Women	1.69 (1.03)	1.35 (1.00)	1.90	n.s.

Note — One male member of the low intelligence group is missing because he lacked the opportunity to report on social service commitments.

TABLE 4.12

*Social Service Commitments for the High
and Low Ideational Productivity Groups*

	High productivity	Low productivity	t	p
Total	1.55 (1.05)	1.35 (1.05)	1.74	n.s.
Men	1.49 (1.08)	1.26 (1.07)	1.56	n.s.
Women	1.63 (1.00)	1.49 (1.00)	0.82	n.s.

Note — One male member of the high productivity group is missing because he lacked the opportunity to report on social service commitments.

TABLE 4.13

*Social Service Commitments for the High and Low
Ideational Uniqueness Groups*

	High uniqueness	Low uniqueness	t	p
Total	1.48 (1.09)	1.37 (1.01)	1.01	n.s.
Men	1.38 (1.14)	1.32 (1.03)	0.37	n.s.
Women	1.64 (1.00)	1.43 (1.00)	1.22	n.s.

displayed by our students. The strong undertone of ethical or humanitarian value concerns which tends to permeate social service activities apparently defines a quality that cuts across the groupings of students which our study contrasts.

Degree of involvement with one's fellow man and with the betterment of his lot is not linked to high or low intelligence status, nor is it linked to the productivity level or the uniqueness of one's ideas. We must confess, as a matter of fact, to deriving some satisfaction from this finding. It argues against trying to make use of cognitive elites, as it were, when defining who will be more likely to show concern for other human beings and who less so. A posture of egalitarianism when it comes to ethical matters hence seems to be one of the implications of the negative results contained in Tables 4.11 through 4.13.

These negative findings have another implication as well. They offer yet another source of evidence supporting the veridicality of the students' reports concerning their nonacademic activities. To the extent that different domains of nonacademic accomplishments manifest theoretically understandable differences in the character of their relationships with the ideational or intellective characteristics under study, we have a further indication that the students' replies to the various queries were made in a meaningful way.

Accomplishments in the field of writing will be considered next. Here is a domain that should provide a clear opportunity for coming to grips with the potential criticism noted earlier. Nonacademic attainments concerning writing might well be expected to reflect the kind of verbal ability tapped by an intelligence index. Such attainments also, however, might well call upon the ability to create plentiful ideas, and ideas that are relatively unique. Recall that all of the statements pertaining to this domain were concerned with one or another kind of writing activity as such: devising original poems, plays, stories, articles, or essays, or functioning as an editor or member of an editorial staff. At issue to at least some degree in all of this, therefore, is the skilled putting together of words for purposes that do not concern the obtaining of higher grades in school.

The findings are quite clear-cut. They are reported in Tables 4.14, 4.15, and 4.16. From Table 4.14 we find that intelligence status, despite its evident verbal facility implications, exerts no effect whatsoever upon writing accomplishments. The overall t value is quite negligible, as are also the t values for the sexes considered separately. Both ideational characteristics, on the other hand, show a strong positive linkage with attainments in the literary field. From Tables 4.15 and 4.16 we find that the overall effects for ideational productivity and uniqueness, respectively, both yield t values significant beyond the .001 level. The latter value is somewhat larger than the former, and shows somewhat greater consistency for the sexes considered separately, but the differences between the productivity and uniqueness effects really are quite minor. The generating of ideas, or the producing of unique ideas in particular, thus has a distinct bearing upon attainments in writing activities carried on outside the academic context. Here is the first instance — and, as it will turn

TABLE 4.14

Writing Accomplishments
for the High and Low Intelligence Groups

	High intelligence	Low intelligence	t	p
Total	1.46 (1.41)	1.47 (1.41)	0.10	n.s.
Men	1.23 (1.22)	1.31 (1.38)	0.43	n.s.
Women	1.81 (1.59)	1.72 (1.42)	0.33	n.s.

Note — One male member of the low intelligence group is missing because he lacked the opportunity to report on writing accomplishments.

TABLE 4.15

Writing Accomplishments for the High and Low Ideational Productivity Groups

	High productivity	Low productivity	t	p
Total	1.85 (1.45)	1.32 (1.29)	3.53	<.001
Men	1.58 (1.44)	1.22 (1.21)	1.91	n.s.
Women	2.25 (1.39)	1.47 (1.41)	3.26	<.01

Note — One male member of the high productivity group is missing because he lacked the opportunity to report on writing accomplishments.

TABLE 4.16

Writing Accomplishments for the High and Low Ideational Uniqueness Groups

	High uniqueness	Low uniqueness	t	p
Total	1.77 (1.36)	1.15 (1.24)	4.36	<.001
Men	1.50 (1.22)	1.06 (1.19)	2.58	<.02
Women	2.18 (1.46)	1.28 (1.31)	3.77	<.001

out, the only one — where ideational uniqueness as such may confer more of an advantage in regard to nonacademic accomplishments than does ideational productivity regardless of uniqueness. Perhaps generating unique ideas is particularly relevant in literary productions. Since, however, output of ideas regardless of uniqueness shows a highly significant over-all effect as well, general resourcefulness in coming up with ideational possibilities once more is found to be important for level of accomplishment in a particular domain of talented activity outside the classroom. The contrast that we have found in the writing domain between the strong positive linkages with ideational output and uniqueness, on the one hand, and the lack of any connection with intelligence level, on the other, seems very impressive indeed.

The potential criticism noted earlier is not supported, therefore, by the findings on literary activities. Intelligence differences turned out to be no more important for writing accomplishments than they did for work in the visual arts or for the exercise of leadership. Even when the kind of talented accomplishment in question penetrates the heartland of the intelligence concept by concerning itself with verbal skills, it is having ideas that counts — not possessing greater facility at manipulating the ideas that may be around.

The results for dramatics are shown in Tables 4.17 through 4.19. Recall that at issue in this domain were accomplishments concerning acting, public speaking, and the technical aspects of dramatic productions. While play-writing was included as a possibility in one item, one could expect that acting in plays, speechmaking, and membership in a play's technical crew would be likely to exhaust most of what students would accomplish in the dramatic arts. Of these possibilities, furthermore, we would expect acting of one kind or another to constitute the most frequently encountered activity of all. Inspection of the tables reveals no significant effects. Intelligence (Table 4.17) once again is of no consequence at all in this domain of nonacademic activity. For output (Table 4.18) and uniqueness (Table 4.19) of ideas, in turn, there are no significant effects either. Breakdowns by sex yielded analogous outcomes. The talents defined by the dramatic arts, therefore, are not functionally related to the groupings contrasted in our tables. Higher intelligence status is of no help in this area, but neither is greater output or uniqueness of ideas. What do these results suggest?

TABLE 4.17

Attainments in Dramatics
for the High and Low Intelligence Groups

	High intelligence	Low intelligence	t	p
Total	1.33 (1.29)	1.35 (1.25)	0.11	n.s.
Men	1.27 (1.34)	1.38 (1.26)	0.59	n.s.
Women	1.43 (1.22)	1.31 (1.25)	0.58	n.s.

Note — One male member of the low intelligence group is missing because he lacked the opportunity to report on attainments in dramatics.

TABLE 4.18

Attainments in Dramatics for the High and Low
Ideational Productivity Groups

	High productivity	Low productivity	t	p
Total	1.56 (1.30)	1.34 (1.26)	1.60	n.s.
Men	1.59 (1.32)	1.29 (1.23)	1.65	n.s.
Women	1.52 (1.26)	1.41 (1.31)	0.50	n.s.

Note — One male member of the high productivity group is missing because he lacked the opportunity to report on attainments in dramatics.

TABLE 4.19

*Attainments in Dramatics for the High and Low
Ideational Uniqueness Groups*

	High uniqueness	Low uniqueness	t	p
Total	1.52 (1.24)	1.31 (1.25)	1.51	n.s.
Men	1.49 (1.31)	1.36 (1.30)	0.68	n.s.
Women	1.56 (1.12)	1.24 (1.19)	1.63	n.s.

The irrelevance of the intelligence contrast simply offers further confirmation for what we have been finding without exception in the case of every domain of nonacademic attainments under investigation: intelligence differences don't matter. Even though verbal skills must be of some relevance to attainments in dramatics, and form a central part of the intelligence concept, the level of verbal skills represented by our low-intelligence groups already is substantial enough that further increments do not add anything useful as far as the dramatic arts are concerned. But what of the negative findings for ideational output and uniqueness? Let us consider the field of dramatics in more detail. When we ask ourselves what it is that most characterizes the dramatic arts, the answer seems to be that this field of endeavor emphasizes performance of what has already been produced — or what we might call reproductive more than innovative modes of functioning. The play, after all, has already been written. Histrionic ability calls upon skill in mimicry, in taking on the behaviors of someone else, in feeling oneself into and successfully portraying the mood or circumstances of another, when using as one's building blocks this already prepared textual material. The orator too is in most cases working from a preformed script. In this regard, acting in a dramatic production seems similar to playing a musical instrument or singing, where again one must be skilled in performance — in reproducing certain characteristics of material that has already been prepared. As the actor works from his script, so the musical performer works from his musical score.

If the reason dramatics shows no significant relationship to the student's capacity for generating many ideas or many unique ideas is that dramatics emphasizes skill at the reproduction of material that has already been written, then we would expect musical activities to show a similar lack of relationship since reproduction of already prepared material is the major focus in that domain as well. This expectation will be tested below. We also might observe that leadership, work in the visual arts, and writing all differ from dramatics and music in that the first three of these areas all involve producing something: the political leader generates plans or guidelines for political action of one kind or another, the artist produces works of art, and the writer produces sentences. Consistent with this point, the three areas in question all exhibited relationships with ideational flow. We would further expect, on the present interpretation, that activity in the area of science once again should show a relationship with ideational resourcefulness, since the devising of one or another kind of experiment or other research project should be the major form taken by nonacademic involvement in science. This expectation too will be the subject of further inquiry below. Finally, the present reasoning leads us to expect that, of the five items in the dramatics domain, the only one that includes any reference at all to the writing of plays should constitute a very small proportion of the activities that are found to take place in this domain. Examination of Table 4.1 confirms this expectation. The item in question is (d) — "received an award for acting, playwriting, or other phase of dramatic production." We see from Table 4.1 that, for any pair of groups, this item accounts for but a tiny proportion (about 4 percent) of the total of the endorsement percentages provided under dramatic arts, so that — as the major kind of innovation possibility included in the items on dramatics — it can have only negligible bearing on the total scores that result. The important points that will require demonstration for the present interpretation to be supported, however, are the expectation of no linkage between either ideational characteristic and accomplishments in music, together with the expected presence of a linkage between one or both ideational characteristics and accomplishments in science.

Before turning to our next domain, that of music, we should point out that the interpretable contrast found between the negative results for dramatics and the positive results for various other domains regarding linkages with ideational characteristics supports once again our assumption that the students' reports on their nonacademic activities are veridical. This view will be even more strongly supported, of course, if the predictions concerning musical and scientific activities that follow from our present interpretation of the results for dramatics are in fact confirmed.

Our inquiries into the field of music dealt, it will be recalled, with such matters as playing a musical instrument, singing, performing with some kind of musical organization, and winning an award in a musical competition. Only one of the six items — item (c) on the list — refers explicitly to the writing of music as distinct from its performance. Reference to Table 4.1 indicates, in turn, that, for any pair of groups, the endorsement percentage for item (c) constitutes a very small proportion (5 or 6 percent) of the total of the endorsement percentages obtained for the musical domain. We note also from Table 4.1 that most of the endorsements in this domain (83 or 84 percent of the total of the endorsement percentages) are provided in response to items (a), (b), and (d), all of which refer explicitly and exclusively to musical performance as distinct from the writing of music. In sum, it is evident that the musical accomplishment scores earned by the students almost entirely reflect skill at the performance of music, not skill at composing. While this is an obvious point in terms of our knowledge of the musical activities carried out by young people in our culture, the point called for documentation because it leads us to expect that musical accomplishments will be unrelated to ideational flow as well as unrelated to intelligence.

Tables 4.20 through 4.22 report the results for music. We find from these tables that all the effects — whether for intelligence, ideational output, or uniqueness — are nil. Separate analyses by sex yielded the same outcomes. The picture that emerges hence is identical to that found in the case of dramatics. Differences regarding flow of ideas as well as differences regarding intelligence level have no consequence for musical accomplishments. The view that dramatics and music will show no linkage with the ideational characteristics under study because both the music and drama fields emphasize performance or reproduction of material already developed by others — rather than the innovating or devising

TABLE 4.20

Musical Accomplishments
for the High and Low Intelligence Groups

	High intelligence	Low intelligence	t	p
Total	1.63 (1.47)	1.65 (1.47)	0.10	n.s.
Men	1.36 (1.52)	1.43 (1.47)	0.36	n.s.
Women	2.04 (1.31)	1.97 (1.42)	0.32	n.s.

TABLE 4.21

Musical Accomplishments for the High and Low
Ideational Productivity Groups

	High productivity	Low productivity	t	p
Total	1.72 (1.50)	1.62 (1.44)	0.61	n.s.
Men	1.42 (1.50)	1.31 (1.41)	0.55	n.s.
Women	2.16 (1.39)	2.09 (1.36)	0.32	n.s.

TABLE 4.22

Musical Accomplishments for the High and Low
Ideational Uniqueness Groups

	High uniqueness	Low uniqueness	t	p
Total	1.60 (1.49)	1.67 (1.48)	0.42	n.s.
Men	1.27 (1.43)	1.47 (1.53)	0.97	n.s.
Women	2.11 (1.46)	1.96 (1.37)	0.62	n.s.

of such material — hence is supported by the findings. The absence of any linkage between musical accomplishments and intelligence also repeats a by now quite familiar story. The two fields among the nonacademic domains under consideration that represented performing arts — dramatics and music — hence provide a consistent pattern which deviates from that found for leadership, work in visual aesthetics, and writing. That the performing arts seem to stand apart from the other nonacademic domains just mentioned offers yet further support for the veridicality of the student report data. But one more domain of nonacademic accomplishments yet awaits our attention: work in the area of science. Will it offer additional support for the present line of reasoning?

Involvement in scientific work outside the academic curriculum was assessed by asking about such matters as whether the student had entered a scientific competition, had constructed a piece of scientific equipment for other than the purposes of a course, had participated in a science club or discussion group, or had won a prize in a state or regional science contest. Has intelligence anything to do with these attainments? The answer from Table 4.23 quite clearly is no. The high and low intelligence groups are about the same in scientific accomplishments. This is true for the sexes considered separately as well as combined. Even though mathematical ability plays such an evident role in our assessment of intelligence and can on obvious grounds be expected to contribute to attainments in scientific pursuits of a nonacademic

TABLE 4.23

*Science Attainments for the High
and Low Intelligence Groups*

	High intelligence	Low intelligence	t	p
Total	1.18 (1.42)	1.11 (1.25)	0.50	n.s.
Men	1.42 (1.50)	1.29 (1.34)	0.61	n.s.
Women	0.82 (1.21)	0.82 (1.06)	0.01	n.s.

kind, the intelligence level of our low intelligence group already is sufficiently high that further intelligence increments make no difference as far as science is concerned. The hypothetical critic mentioned earlier who expected intelligence to make a contribution to nonacademic attainments in writing and science hence receives a disappointment not only in the former case but also in the latter.

What about the effects of ideational productivity and uniqueness on science attainments? The results are presented in Tables 4.24 and 4.25, respectively. A strong relationship is found between output of ideas and science attainments, significant overall beyond the .001 level (Table 4.24). A less strong, but still significant, overall relationship appears between ideational uniqueness and science attainments (Table 4.25). With the effect arising from the ideational productivity contrast stronger overall and more consistent for the separate sexes than the effect arising from the uniqueness contrast, it is evident that the former effect is the more basic. Resourcefulness in coming up with ideas plays a strong and pervasive role in scientific attainments outside the classroom, while level of intelligence in our sample does not.

TABLE 4.24

Science Attainments for the High and Low
Ideational Productivity Groups

	High productivity	Low productivity	*t*	*p*
Total	1.37 (1.44)	0.85 (1.07)	3.79	<.001
Men	1.58 (1.54)	1.01 (1.19)	2.94	<.01
Women	1.06 (1.23)	0.60 (0.83)	2.53	<.02

TABLE 4.25

*Science Attainments for the High and Low
Ideational Uniqueness Groups*

	High uniqueness	Low uniqueness	t	p
Total	1.29 (1.41)	0.93 (1.11)	2.60	<.01
Men	1.45 (1.49)	1.14 (1.19)	1.62	n.s.
Women	1.05 (1.26)	0.62 (0.90)	2.27	<.05

Let us take next a somewhat different perspective toward the present chapter's findings: namely, a brief examination of the data on an item-by-item basis. It is of interest to inquire, in the case of those domains where overall effects were obtained, whether the effects were sufficiently pervasive to be reflected even at the level of single items. This is an extremely stringent test, of course, since one is referring to the presence or absence of only a single type of accomplishment behavior at a time. Despite the stringency, however, the same general picture emerged. The domains in question are, of course, leadership, art, writing, and science. We shall describe the item findings for the sexes combined in order to maximize the possible frequency for the occurrence of any single type of accomplishment behavior, but similar results also are found for the sexes taken separately.

Consider first the high and low ideational output groups. Table 4.26 presents the data. A significant positive association (beyond the .05 level or better by a χ^2 test) between ideational productivity and proportion of endorsements is found for three of the four leadership items, all four of the art items, three of the six writing items, and five of the

TABLE 4.26

*Percentage of High and Low Ideational Productivity Groups
Endorsing Each Self-descriptive Item*

Item	High productivity ($N = 167$)	Low productivity ($N = 169$)	χ^2	p
Leadership				
(a)	98	92	5.75	<.02
(b)	92	79	11.07	<.001
(c)	58	39	11.43	<.001
(d)	16	14	0.25	n.s.
Art				
(a)	43	24	13.38	<.001
(b)	17	7	8.26	<.01
(c)	12	5	4.71	<.05
(d)	7	2	5.77	<.02
Social Service				
(a)	78	71	2.36	n.s.
(b)	49	46	0.35	n.s.
(c)	27	18	4.22	<.05
Writing				
(a)	52	29	18.12	<.001
(b)	43	31	5.19	<.05
(c)	13	7	4.29	<.05
(d)	11	8	0.94	n.s.
(e)	45	40	0.84	n.s.
(f)	21	17	0.61	n.s.
Drama				
(a)	54	47	1.32	n.s.
(b)	61	52	2.62	n.s.
(c)	24	20	0.78	n.s.
(d)	8	4	2.63	n.s.
(e)	10	11	0.09	n.s.

TABLE 4.26 (continued)

Percentage of High and Low Ideational Productivity Groups Endorsing Each Self-descriptive Item

Item	High productivity (N = 167)	Low productivity (N = 169)	χ^2	p
Music				
(a)	58	53	1.00	n.s.
(b)	40	37	0.29	n.s.
(c)	10	8	0.64	n.s.
(d)	46	45	0.01	n.s.
(e)	14	14	0.04	n.s.
(f)	4	6	1.00	n.s.
Science				
(a)	40	28	5.16	<.05
(b)	22	12	5.72	<.02
(c)	20	11	6.05	<.02
(d)	37	26	4.30	<.05
(e)	9	1	10.63	<.01
(f)	10	7	1.01	n.s.

Note — For social service, writing, and drama, one member of the high productivity group is missing because he lacked the opportunity to report on these domains. The χ^2 tests in Tables 4.26, 4.27, and 4.28 compare the frequencies of endorsements and nonendorsements for the two groups in question.

six science items. In the writing domain, two of the three items that failed to yield a significant association were the only two that referred to editorial work — items (e) and (f) — rather than referring more explicitly to creative forms of writing. If anything, then, this outcome actually serves to reinforce our earlier interpretation. Consider next the high and low ideational uniqueness groups. The results appear in Table 4.27. By the same statistical criterion of a χ^2 value beyond the .05 level or better, a significant positive associa-

TABLE 4.27

*Percentage of High and Low Ideational Uniqueness Groups
Endorsing Each Self-descriptive Item*

Item	High uniqueness ($N = 166$)	Low uniqueness ($N = 167$)	χ^2	p
Leadership				
(a)	96	93	2.08	n.s.
(b)	86	80	1.65	n.s.
(c)	52	46	1.08	n.s.
(d)	15	13	0.25	n.s.
Art				
(a)	43	23	15.02	<.001
(b)	18	7	8.16	<.01
(c)	10	5	3.56	n.s.
(d)	6	2	2.72	n.s.
Social Service				
(a)	74	74	0.00	n.s.
(b)	48	46	0.07	n.s.
(c)	27	17	5.20	<.05
Writing				
(a)	52	26	24.86	<.001
(b)	40	24	9.59	<.01
(c)	10	5	2.16	n.s.
(d)	12	8	1.70	n.s.
(e)	46	36	3.76	n.s.
(f)	17	16	0.03	n.s.
Drama				
(a)	52	46	1.32	n.s.
(b)	58	52	1.62	n.s.
(c)	25	20	1.15	n.s.
(d)	9	4	4.17	<.05
(e)	7	10	0.98	n.s.

TABLE 4.27 (continued)

Percentage of High and Low Ideational Uniqueness Groups Endorsing Each Self-descriptive Item

Item	High uniqueness (N = 166)	Low uniqueness (N = 167)	χ^2	p
Music				
(a)	54	55	0.00	n.s.
(b)	39	38	0.02	n.s.
(c)	10	9	0.04	n.s.
(d)	43	45	0.15	n.s.
(e)	11	15	0.90	n.s.
(f)	3	5	1.17	n.s.
Science				
(a)	38	31	2.03	n.s.
(b)	22	15	2.51	n.s.
(c)	22	9	10.36	<.01
(d)	31	29	0.26	n.s.
(e)	8	4	3.46	n.s.
(f)	8	6	0.44	n.s.

tion is found for none of the four leadership items, two of the four art items, two of the six writing items, and one of the six science items. Turning finally in Table 4.28 to the high and low intelligence groups and applying the same statistical criterion once again, a significant positive association is found for none of the four leadership items, none of the four art items, none of the six writing items, and only one of the six science items. None of the 60 tests just described yielded significant reversals except for two of those involving intelligence: in the case of one leadership item and one writing item, the high intelligence group actually manifested a significantly lower proportion of endorsements than the low intelligence group.

TABLE 4.28

*Percentage of High and Low Intelligence Groups
Endorsing Each Self-descriptive Item*

Item	High intelligence ($N = 168$)	Low intelligence ($N = 170$)	χ^2	p
Leadership				
(a)	92	94	0.21	n.s.
(b)	82	84	0.23	n.s.
(c)	44	55	4.28	<.05
(d)	12	13	0.08	n.s.
Art				
(a)	32	37	1.14	n.s.
(b)	9	12	1.04	n.s.
(c)	5	7	0.19	n.s.
(d)	3	4	0.32	n.s.
Social Service				
(a)	75	71	0.68	n.s.
(b)	51	40	4.53	<.05
(c)	20	22	0.14	n.s.
Writing				
(a)	36	36	0.01	n.s.
(b)	37	30	2.03	n.s.
(c)	12	8	1.69	n.s.
(d)	10	8	0.16	n.s.
(e)	36	48	4.67	<.05
(f)	16	18	0.31	n.s.
Drama				
(a)	42	48	1.34	n.s.
(b)	57	51	1.09	n.s.
(c)	21	24	0.57	n.s.
(d)	6	4	0.58	n.s.
(e)	8	8	0.05	n.s.

TABLE 4.28 (continued)

Percentage of High and Low Intelligence Groups
Endorsing Each Self-descriptive Item

Item	High intelligence ($N = 168$)	Low intelligence ($N = 170$)	χ^2	p
Music				
(a)	54	54	0.01	n.s.
(b)	39	35	0.42	n.s.
(c)	9	8	0.05	n.s.
(d)	47	49	0.11	n.s.
(e)	11	14	0.60	n.s.
(f)	4	4	0.07	n.s.
Science				
(a)	30	36	1.16	n.s.
(b)	18	22	0.81	n.s.
(c)	12	15	0.83	n.s.
(d)	34	27	1.88	n.s.
(e)	10	5	2.77	n.s.
(f)	14	5	6.95	<.01

Note — For social service, writing, and drama, one member of the low intelligence group is missing because he lacked the opportunity to report on these domains.

Taking the 20 items in the four domains together, then, the ideational productivity contrast yielded significant positive associations for 15 of the 20, the ideational uniqueness contrast yielded significant positive associations for 5 of the 20, and the intelligence contrast yielded significant positive associations for only one of the 20. The other 5 items for ideational productivity all yielded positive trends, the other 15 items for ideational uniqueness all yielded positive trends, and the other 19 items for intelligence yielded the two significant reversals already noted, 5 positive trends, and

12 negative trends. Thus, the direction of the association with intelligence for 14 of the 20 items actually was negative. What of the item results for the three domains — social service, music, and dramatics — where no overall effects were obtained? Of the 14 items in question, associations with ideational productivity (Table 4.26) are nonsignificant for 13 of the 14, associations with ideational uniqueness (Table 4.27) are nonsignificant for 12 of the 14, and associations with intelligence (Table 4.28) are nonsignificant for 13 of the 14. In all respects, then, analyses at the item level completely confirm the analyses presented earlier by domain.

While our concern in this volume is with evaluating the concept of general intelligence, because that is the concept which is customarily invoked in our culture for answering questions about talent, it might also be noted that breaking the concept down into its verbal ability and mathematical ability components yielded about the same picture as has been described for the concept as a whole. Thus, men scoring in the upper and lower thirds for their sex on verbal SAT scores were compared by t tests for accomplishment levels in each of the seven nonacademic domains under study and also for generality of nonacademic accomplishments. Comparable analyses were conducted for women scoring in the upper and lower thirds for their sex on verbal SAT scores, for men using mathematical SAT scores on a within-sex basis as the means for defining upper and lower thirds, for women using mathematical SAT scores in the same manner, for the sexes combined on a within-sex basis into upper and lower thirds on verbal SAT scores, and for the sexes combined in the same way into upper and lower thirds on mathematical SAT scores. With t tests run for each of the seven nonacademic domains and for generality of nonacademic accomplishments as well, we thus have a total of 48 tests in all: six comparisons for each of eight measures. Of the 48 tests, only one difference between means reached the .05 level of significance in the direction of a positive relationship between an SAT comparison and a measure of nonacademic attainments: for women, high mathematical SAT scorers excelled low mathematical SAT scorers in level of social service attainments. As a matter of fact, three other scattered tests actually yielded differences between means that reached the .05 level in the opposite direction — that is, a negative relationship between an SAT comparison and a measure of nonacademic attainments. The obvious conclusion is that, for the present set of comparisons as before, intelligence measures are unrelated to indicators of talented nonacademic accomplishments.

The implications of intelligence, ideational output, and ideational uniqueness for the various realms of talented nonacademic accomplishments that we have investigated now seem clear. The hypotheses with which this book began have received strong confirmation, and in addition a separation has been sharpened between kinds of nonacademic accomplishments that draw upon talents for innovating or producing something, and kinds that do not. First of all, high versus low intelligence status in our sample — although powerfully related to traditional forms of academic achievement, as we saw in Chapter 3 — is clearly *not* related to attainments in any of the nonacademic domains that we have studied. High versus low intelligence status also is quite unrelated to generality of nonacademic accomplishments across the various domains as a whole. These statements hold for the college student sample in general — they are as true for the members of one sex as for the members of the other. Since the nonacademic attainments that we have considered are valuable on their face — that is, since they are of undeniable worth to the society — it is sobering to discover that intelligence status in our sample very consistently shows no linkage with these attainments.

Resourcefulness in generating ideas or what we have called ideational productivity, on the other hand, displays a very strong linkage with these attainments. It does so when we consider generality of nonacademic accomplishments without regard to specific area, and it also does so when we consider level of accomplishment in particular domains that share a common emphasis upon innovation: namely, leadership, art, writing, and science. The relationships in all these cases were very clear in terms of statistical strength and again were quite consistent for the members of both sexes. It looks as if the ability to express a greater number of possibilities in one's thought (Wallach, 1967) plays a pivotal role across a range of talented pursuits that extends from the devising of political strategems and plans for political action in student organizations, through the making of paintings or drawings and the writing of poetry or prose, to the innovating of plans for scientific research. It is involvements in these particular areas, then, that make the major contribution to the finding that ideational productivity level also is related to generality of nonacademic accomplishments as a whole. When, by contrast, we consider social service commitments, dramatics, and music, no linkage with ideational productivity emerges. The reason in the first case seems to be that degree of humanitarian concern for one's fellow man draws upon wellsprings of a different order than pursuits of a more innovative kind, and perhaps it is just as well that persons capable of generating a richer flow of ideas should fail to have a monopoly on ethical sensitivity. Dramatics and music, in turn, were found to emphasize performance or reproduction of material already produced by others, and it is apparently because of the importance of performance rather than innovative skills in these areas that they too failed to show any linkage with the capacity to produce larger numbers of ideas.

What about the production of unique ideas in particular? By and large, the evidence suggests that it is ideational output in general, rather than uniqueness as such, that plays the pivotal role for nonacademic accomplishments. Here is the balance sheet. Output was more strongly related than uniqueness to generality of nonacademic accomplishments, and to attainments in science. Output alone, not uniqueness at all, was related to the exercise of leadership. Output and uniqueness both were strongly related to attainments in art. Only in the case of writing activities was uniqueness more strongly linked than output to level of accomplishment, but the relationship for output was quite strong here as well. Finally, neither uniqueness nor output showed relationships with social service commitments or with attainments in dramatics or music. These findings clearly point to the conclusion that level of ideational output in general, rather than producing unique ideas in particular, is what matters most for the non-academic attainments under investigation. Recalling our consideration of underlying processes in Chapter 1, the implication is that what distinguishes the students who show stronger accomplishments in these nonacademic domains is more on the order of greater cognitive energy, or a higher typical level of ideational activity, or, if you will, greater cognitive vitality - - rather than a greater specific urge for novelty or uniqueness as such.

Intelligence within the range of the present sample does not matter, but resourcefulness in producing ideas does, when it comes to talented accomplishments outside the classroom. Before turning to a discussion of the implications of this general finding, let us look in more detail at some examples of the students whom we have been describing thus far en masse.

Chapter **5**

Some Individual Students

By now we have come to understand in quantitative terms certain generalizations about thinking characteristics on the one hand, and academic and nonacademic kinds of accomplishments on the other, pertaining to our sample of students. We also conducted brief interviews with some of the students from the sample. The basis for deciding whom to interview simply was an interest in representing among our interviewees the diversity of cognitive characteristics which we had measured for the sample as a whole, together with the interviewee's willingness to volunteer. Why conduct interviews? Since interview materials are notoriously unruly, how could one expect a casual conversation with an interviewee to prove enlightening with regard to the specific questions addressed in this research? Despite this problem, we hoped that some qualitative differences might be detectable if we considered persons who exemplified sufficiently extreme positions regarding the thinking characteristics under study. If so, then the generalizations documented by the quantitative data would become all the richer.

The interviewer — a psychology graduate student — had a quite straightforward task. Without knowing the intelligence, ideational productivity, or ideational uniqueness status of any student whom he interviewed, he was to start the discussion — conducted at the beginning of the student's sophomore year of college — with a single, general question: "As you look back on your first year at college, what strike you as the most important or the most meaningful experiences you have had thus far?" The conversation then was to proceed with minimum direction or intervention on his part. After about half an hour, he was to bring the conversation to a close. From the tape recording of the conversation, made with the student's full knowledge since the recording machine sat before him on a table as he spoke, the interviewer then was to prepare a sketch summarizing the interview. These sketches form the basis of the accounts provided in the present chapter.

Our purpose in providing some detailed sketches of particular individuals thus is to point up at a naturalistic level the contrast that we have been able to document between the psychological import of intelligence and of ideational output. Recall our basic findings: that intelligence level, much more than ideational output or uniqueness, predicts the student's degree of academic achievement; but that ideational output in particular, and intelligence level not at all, predicts the student's attainments in a variety of talented pursuits outside the classroom. The directive provided by these findings is a clear one when it comes to naturalistic observation. A contrast between students high and low in ideational productivity should look different from a parallel contrast between students high and low regarding intelligence. This point guided us, then, in our presentation of interview materials. We applied an objective rule for selecting which interviews to report upon — a rule whose aim was to distill from among our interviewees those who would represent the closest approximation to the extremes with respect to ideational output or intelligence. The rule was this. Among the men whom we interviewed, we chose the following four students: the man with the highest index score for his sex on ideational output, the man with the lowest index score for his sex on ideational output, the man with the highest index score for his sex on intelligence, and the man with the lowest index score for his sex on intelligence. We proceeded analogously for the women. Application of this rule provided us with eight students, and it is upon them that we comment in the paragraphs that follow. They are those students among our interviewees who obtained the upper and the lower extreme scores on ideational fluency and on intelligence, determined on a within-sex basis. Note further that, in all cases, the upper or lower extreme score in question also was quite extreme in terms of the sample as a whole for the students of the same sex.

What, then, were these maximally extreme interviewees like? Our order of presentation was: first, the man and the woman interviewees highest in ideational output; next, the man and the woman interviewees lowest in ideational output; third, the highest intelligence scorers among the men and among the women interviewees; and last, the man and the woman interviewees scoring lowest regarding intelligence. The names we used were, of course, pseudonyms. Furthermore, any descriptive material that might possibly have been revealing of individual identity was eliminated or was changed in such a manner as to make identification impossible while still preserving the original psychological mood.

The highest ideational output scorer among our male interviewees was John. Compared with the male research sample as a whole, his ideational output score was sixth from the top; his intelligence score, on the other hand, was middling. John had been involved in important leadership and managerial roles in student government and student organizations.

He was a political science major, but felt "up in the air" occupationally at the point of the interview. "I want to do something with people . . . but I don't know how to best use my talents yet." Work in student government had meant a great deal to John. "I think the lessons you learn in student government are things you can use no matter what you do the rest of your life . . . you know, about giving it all you have, being fair, working with others toward a common goal." In terms of viewing the future, John felt that he would like to do something that would help teach others to find meaningful lives in the society. He felt that he could be most useful in this way because "I don't have a technical mind. . . . There are still people needed to teach values and not numbers." His involvement with student government was, in his estimation, providing him with invaluable experience concerning how to organize and administer various kinds of programs and policies. The political leadership aspects of the student government work came closest, in fact, to defining his idea of what life is all about: " . . . the idea of victory or defeat, character building, how you react to various situations . . . it's accepting a challenge."

There was a strong emphasis on the practical in John; on wanting to get things done in the real world, through organizing the activities of others toward attaining one or another useful goal. At the time of the interview, however, he was unsure of his focus beyond this general commitment to activism. "Whenever I saw somebody talking about a crisis of self-identity, I could never picture that happening to me because I was pretty confident and probably confident in an unthinking way. . . . Last year I realized how much potential I have and how little I have used of it." " . . . I'm unsure about a lot of things . . . and I guess I worry a lot about the future." He felt an urgent need "to do something," and hence was not interested in extended education. He wasn't really sure what he meant when he viewed himself as undergoing a crisis in his self-identity, but somehow did not feel that he was doing all the things he could be doing. One got the feeling of someone itching to have effects upon the practical world. Yet he was doing much in that direction already.

As far as academic work was concerned, his courses did not seem to constitute an arena of great affective significance for him, although he did well enough. His remarking that he had received grades that he considered to be too high suggested something of this dispassionateness toward the academic. One came away with the impression that while course work posed no particular problem for him, neither did it provide him with anything like the degree of meaning and personal definition that he derived from his student government work.

Sally scored highest in ideational productivity among our female interviewees. She also was the top scorer on ideational output compared with the female research sample as a whole, while scoring relatively low on intelligence. Sally's reaction to her freshman academic experience was disappointment at the system of courses and grades. "I didn't like the kind of strict categorization of things." As she saw it, college consisted of only " . . . falling asleep in lecture, getting D's and F's", and she didn't feel that defining learning in terms of an assorted sampling of lecture courses was fair. She came to feel that " . . . somebody didn't have the same sense of balance that I did, and I was pretty sure that mine was right." Among academic subjects, she was most attracted to art. "I really resent having to be a 'broadened' student . . . I am pretty interested in art courses . . . I really hate things like math." Sally liked art because of " . . . images — it's so great, it's totally an imaginary flight, I just get carried away." She wasn't interested in art as a stepping stone toward teaching or any other career; rather, "Art just intrigues me."

Sally's antagonism to the standard structure of courses and exams during her first year in college kept her in pretty much of a constant stew. The quarrels she felt with the academic system left her without time or inclination to carry on the sculpture work which she had previously done with great enjoyment. In describing her state of mind when she was embroiled in mental battles with the system, she said, "I get all upset and don't have time to sculpt." These days, however, she was trying to forget her grievances against the academic side of college. Instead of fretting over her feelings of dissatisfaction with the academic situation, which she saw no real way of making into something more meaningful for herself, she was trying to base her self-definition upon doing sculpture and upon meaningful interpersonal relationships. This shift of focus seemed to be working, in that she reported herself to be happy now and feeling like involving herself in sculpture again for the first time since her arrival at college.

In her discussion of the preceding matters, Sally impressed the interviewer as highly spontaneous, extremely expressive, and possessing a lively sense of humor. Particularly intriguing to the interviewer was Sally's way of coming to terms with the school setting. Having experienced difficulty in adjusting to an academic situation which in many ways constrained her from the spontaneity and direct expressiveness which she found natural, she was seeking to shift the arena from which she derived personal meaning and self-definition away from academics and toward particular friendships and extracurricular sculpture work. As far as the interviewer could tell, this shift in her primary sources of meaning had been made with remarkable ease.

Next we turn to the opposite end of the ideational output dimension. Of the male interviewees, Bob scored lowest on productivity of ideas. Considering the male research sample as a whole, his ideational output score was second from the bottom, while his intelligence score was middling. For Bob, a big issue the first year in college was earning sufficiently high grades to be thought well of by his family. He studied more than average, and had been satisfied with his academic standing. Bob had considered going to business school after finishing college. "A Master's degree from a good business school is pretty good assurance . . . There are millions of fields open." At times he questioned whether all the academic grinding was worth it — "cramming facts into my head." He wondered how much he would study if he didn't need the grades to get into a good business school. However, he didn't feel that the academic side of things should be made any easier, because then it wouldn't be worth as much to be able to say that he got his degree from Duke. It was evident, then, that external standards of approval constituted very important values for Bob. His academic work seemed motivated very specifically in terms of his need for current social approval and in terms of his future career plans. The latter, in turn, were premised upon his achieving a position that would insure sufficient social status.

Regarding more general matters, Bob said that he was disappointed by the high degree of liberalism that he found on campus. He was worried about the kind of name this would give the university, feeling that if it became too liberal he would be ashamed to admit later on that this was where he had gone to college. Once again, then, he was defining his academic situation in social image and social status terms.

Ruth was the female interviewee who scored lowest on ideational productivity. Compared with the total female research sample, she scored fourth from the bottom in ideational productivity and was middling regarding intelligence. Insecurity seemed to be the main feature of Ruth's self-presentation. She described herself in the college environment as tending to wait for others to initiate conversations and as being somewhat fearful of expressing her views. Her attitude toward academic study was that it is necessary, but she had rarely been intrigued by the subject matter. She gave one the impression, as a matter of fact, that she saw course work as a bitter pill that must be swallowed because it has beneficial long-range consequences. She most preferred courses that are logical and precise — where the structure of the material is very explicit so that a clear distinction is present between what is right and what is wrong. Her approach to learning was a passive one in which she waited for the teacher to inspire her and create interest. By and large, this had not tended to happen for her, and Ruth's general response had been one of withdrawal.

What of the intelligence contrast? Of the male interviewees, the student with the highest intelligence score was Reed. His intelligence score was third from the top for the male research sample as a whole, while his ideational output score was middling. Reed studied a reasonable amount and came out reasonably well academically. As far as a career is concerned, Reed had made up his mind: he planned to go on to law school. History and literature courses had never been much trouble for him. His academic aptitudes, some work the previous summer helping out in a legal office, and a feeling that he should do something relating to people, had led to his deciding upon a career in law. Armed with this career decision and holding his own academically with a medium amount of studying, he found himself with free time on his hands.

Reed tended to fritter away this free time in a random fashion. "I sleep a lot . . . Mostly I just goof around." Apart from the times when he was studying, he floated around the dorm talking to people without feeling this to be a particularly meaningful activity. He was vaguely dissatisfied with this goofing around, but didn't really seem to know what to do about it. In commenting on this matter, he noted that being oriented in terms of his future career goals left him with a kind of vacuum as far as the present is concerned, " . . . and that's why some of the time I'm not doing anything." In sum, Reed seemed pretty much to be coasting along, neither feeling nor seeking much challenge from the environment.

The person with the highest intelligence score among our female interviewees was Norma. She also was the highest scorer on intelligence for the female research sample as a whole, and was middling on ideational productivity. Norma saw herself as bored and lazy. "I'm just sitting here and taking courses and doing nothing . . . and you get fed up with it." She sounded tired of the entire academic system — tired of worrying about grades, worrying about getting into graduate school, worrying about whether her professors thought well of her, worrying about striving to get pieces of paper attesting to academic excellence. Yet she also saw herself as cowardly. "I'm too chicken to quit school. . . . I think a lot of this has to do with myself. I'm pretty satisfied here and that's what makes me mad because I'm complacent."

Upon further discussion, Norma came to feel that the issue was not really whether one has the guts to quit school or not, but rather what one does in any environment. Norma was concerned that she did not have the drive to work for things that she considered really important, but rather fell into maintaining the status quo for herself as a path of least resistance. While noting that she was very interested in literature, for example, she went on to say that she did not do any writing herself. She tended to feel as a personal deficiency that, while she knew she had a mind, she was not really concerned about anything. Although she realized that she should "quit complaining and do something," she seemed unable to galvanize herself. Instead, she continued on in the same way as before — somewhat aware of her present confusion but responding primarily with apathy and resignation. As she put it, "I commit myself mostly to my friends."

Consider finally two students at the low end of the intelligence distribution. Frank was the student with the lowest intelligence score among our male interviewees. His intelligence standing also was the lowest compared with the male research sample as a whole, while his ideational output level was middling. Frank spent his first college year worrying about grades and, as a result, "studying like hell." The outcome was a respectable grade point average. This year he had been having more of a good time and found that he was "not quite as worried" about his academic situation. "I used to be superconscientious . . . So far this year it's been real easy . . . I feel a little guilty about this fun." Frank had been enjoying the living group side of college: he felt comfortable with his dormitory friends and found these social relationships to be an important part of his college life. The issue of how his peers view him had, however, been a continuing source of concern and insecurity for Frank. Becoming accepted by others had been an important goal of his conduct. Having spent a period of intensive worry about this acceptance, he now felt more confident of his social situation and as a result was exhibiting greater involvement than before in campus social activities.

Frank had been finding himself seeking answers to his religious questions lately, but the character of his interest seemed to hinge upon issues of personal insecurity once again. "I guess this is concerned about whether I'm saved or not." Regarding career plans, he felt drawn to computer technology. The appeal of computer work for him seemed to arise from the chance it provided for solving logical puzzles. In addition, computer technology attracted him because it offered a relatively new frontier of application, and Frank also noted that his family was enthusiastic about the idea of his going into this area. He seemed pretty much set in his occupational choice and satisfied with it. One suspects, however, that this decisiveness with respect to career plans, as well as other aspects of his present conduct, may be heavily oriented toward controlling feelings of insecurity.

Among the women whom we interviewed, the individual with the lowest intelligence score was Anne. Compared with the female research sample as a whole, she stood third from the bottom on intelligence and was middling on ideational output. College had been a broadening experience for Anne. Her views of herself and others had been influenced considerably through exposure to a much more diversified set of peers than had been available to her before college. Anne felt that she has gotten a great deal out of relationships with people unlike herself — people who are forceful and dynamic; they " . . . say definite things about everything. Well, most of the time I'm a listener, and most of the time they're the talker . . . but I like to challenge them when they're talking." Anne said that she was still in the process of thinking over the new ideas to which she had been exposed. Another aspect of the social environment that meant a lot to Anne was whether people were sincere or not. As a result of her freshman year experiences she now found it easier to relate to people and to discover what they are genuinely like. Attaining this kind of interpersonal openness means that " . . . you have to reveal yourself, but you get so much back too."

In regard to academic matters, Anne viewed herself as follows: "I'm not real, real smart but I just want to learn how to use what I have." She currently is mulling over the choice of a major, and would like it to be something that will give her competence " . . . to do something definite." All in all, Anne seemed to be taking in a variety of new experiences in a relatively open manner. How much impact these experiences will have on her actual conduct, however, remains unclear.

We have considered the life situations of eight students. How are these young people faring? Perhaps the matter that stands out most prominently is the variation among them in the degree of personal meaningfulness which they are presently experiencing. John and Sally, the two high ideational output students, seem to be best off in this regard. John is heavily committed to his leadership activities, Sally to her sculpture. Both have their existential problems, to be sure, but they approach them with maturity. They are realistically attuned to the limitations of the strictly academic: John finds the latter sphere too detached from the real world, while Sally smarts under the imposition of what she perceives as unreasonable approaches to learning. The challenge, of course, is so to structure academic work that it has more to offer people of this kind.

For Bob and Ruth, the low ideational output students, academic work also seems unappealing — but for what strike us as the wrong reasons. Their approach to course work is rather extrinsic and concrete: a person studies because it gets him through college, and graduating from college is a necessary thing to do. The purposes which motivate them are immature ones — to get the degree, to be thought well of by others. Little direct meaning seems to inhere in what they are doing.

On the whole, the high and low intelligence students seem less discriminable into two types than the high and low ideational output students. Reed and Norma, the two high intelligence students, are bothered by ennui and boredom. They are doing the kinds of things that the culture expects of them — getting acceptable grades or planning a specific career — but they are left feeling empty and they cannot effectively put their finger on why. The malaise doesn't really become formulated in a constructive way so that it might eventuate in positive action.

The two low intelligence students, Frank and Anne, both seem relatively involved in social relationships, but the girl seems more secure about these matters than the boy. As with Reed, Frank's specificity of career objectives may well be in the service of reducing insecurity. Anne seems relatively happy, but has yet to come to grips in an active way with any of the new perspectives upon life that she has encountered from those around her.

If one asks which of the eight students show the highest degrees of competence at self-initiated activities — that is, at activities which seem more to arise as a response to self-generated demands rather than as a response to environmental pressures — the answer again seems to be John and Sally, the students of high ideational output. Both seem to be in reasonably good touch with their talents, and to be oriented toward fulfilling them. Sally's path in this regard, however, seems to have been considerably more rocky than that of John. In any case, both possess strong competencies that seem to arise quite genuinely from their natures. By contrast, all the other students, with the exception of Anne, appear to be burdened in one way or another by society's expectations, as mediated by family or school. Much of their time is spent doing things with the aim of maintaining or gaining a sense of self-worth by behaving as others think they should. They want academic success because the society rewards them for it, but little by way of intrinsic meaning seems attached to their academic work. Problems of insecurity and meaninglessness are more explicit for some of them, more implicit for others. Anne, finally, seems relatively free of these problems but nevertheless has protected herself thus far through maintaining a passive stance. What we have found, of course, pertains to a particular contextual setting which these students were sharing. Were they in a different context, other contrasts among them might have been highlighted.

Even at the level of an open-ended conversation, then, intelligence contrasts and ideational productivity contrasts suggest quite different patterns of human experience and conduct. Since the interviewer did not know the status of his interviewees with regard to intelligence or the ideational characteristics under study, and since the eight persons here described were selected for presentation on a basis quite independent of the content of the interviews themselves, these accounts of individual students offer further support for the psychological meaningfulness of distinguishing ideational productivity from intelligence.

Chapter **6**

_____

Implications of the Findings

There is little doubt that many if not most college students wear their SAT standing as a kind of prisoner identification number. Having internalized their society's ideology to the effect that a person's intelligence level represents the best estimate that can be made of his potential for meaningful contributions to the environment, it inevitably follows that their SAT status — an incontrovertible index of general intelligence — becomes of great significance in their lives. They cannot, of course, be blamed for this attitude. Their society reinforces it at every turn. They know, for example, that, if they wish to go to graduate school, they will have to perform well on what amounts to another intelligence test all over again — such as the verbal and mathematical aptitude sections of the Graduate Record Examination, or the Miller Analogies Test, or both. Why is this information used in making decisions about the candidate's qualifications? Perhaps most importantly, because such intelligence assessors show substantial linkages with future grades. But what else do they show linkages with? Certainly not with any of the definitions of talented nonacademic accomplishments that we pursued in the present investigation. And these included such matters as work in science and in writing, not just matters which are further from the traditional conception of the academy such as painting pictures or exercising political leadership. What, in turn, are grades good for? The evidence at best is ambiguous, but if one were interested, say, in predicting who would turn out to be among the creative writers of the next generation, one certainly would be well advised to consider not only past grades in school but also, and perhaps much more importantly, evidence of past attainments in writing carried on outside the classroom. In our sample of students, intelligence test scores pointed to those who earned higher grades but did not point to those who displayed higher levels of such writing attainments.

Substantially related to such writing attainments, on the other hand — and also to other kinds of nonacademic pursuits in which innovating or producing something plays a major role — was the person's facility in generating a plentiful supply of ideas. Students seem to vary in a general way among themselves with regard to activity of an idea-producing kind. Those whose typical stance is to be productive of many ideas give evidence of stronger nonacademic attainments in leadership, art, writing, and science — and even, as a matter of fact, earn somewhat higher grades as well — than those whose typical posture is to be productive of few ideas. With intelligence unrelated to these and other forms of nonacademic attainments, and with an independent assessment of what may best be understood as a person's cognitive energy level or degree of cognitive vitality showing strong relationships with a variety of accomplishments outside the classroom, it is evident that intelligence ought not to have a monopoly when it comes to assessing a student's talent potential. The kinds of nonacademic accomplishments that we investigated may, after all, represent a much better basis for predicting what students will go on to do in the life that starts when schooling is over than is offered by the academic grades they have earned. Can we afford, then, to ignore the evidence provided by the accomplishments themselves, as well as by the idea-producing ability that seems to serve as a generic cognitive substrate for many of them? Evidence of these kinds should, it seems to us, receive at least as much weight as does intelligence level when it comes to providing further opportunities to young people for talent development.

A case in point will help to make the practical issues clear. Let us return to the matter of selecting from among college student applicants those who will be admitted for graduate school work — or those who will be granted a scholarship for attendance in graduate school. The typical committee procedure for deciding who will be admitted or who will be offered scholarship support — and we have sat on our fair share of such committees — ends up giving great weight to the numbers that represent the student's general intelligence standing: his Graduate Record Examination aptitude test scores, for example, or these plus his Miller Analogies Test scores as well, if both types of test credentials were requested from the applicant. Beyond the already mentioned fact of their power to predict future grade attainments, heavy emphasis is given to these test scores for several additional reasons as well. First of all, just because they are numbers; that is, they provide a ready yardstick for making comparisons between applicants. The student at the 86th percentile on an intellective aptitude test can be discriminated from the student at the 84th percentile. Secondly, because their meaning has been arrived at in terms of a national frame of reference, so that they provide an assessment basis which presumably is fair to all, rather than, for example, favoring the student from a school whose teachers make it a habit to write more extensive letters of recommendation. Third, these numbers are expected to reflect general intelligence, and hence to indicate the candidate's genuine potential or aptitude — what he would be capable of if he were to fulfill the talent that is within him — rather than just what he may have achieved academically thus far. In this way it is expected that discrimination against late bloomers will be avoided. Since these intelligence scores tend to relate to subsequent grade achievement in graduate school, and this, after all, is the academician's main way of evaluating student success, the committee tends to be reinforced more often than it is punished for its reliance upon the scores. The greatest ultimate contribution, however, may well be expected to arise from the student of high ideational productivity regardless of intelligence level within the college student range. This is the student who already has exerted a general innovative impact upon his environment, and it may be a good bet to expect that he will continue in that vein.

In a nutshell, the situation that we have arrived at with respect to the definition of human talent seems to be this. As soon as one looks outside the classroom for evidences of talented accomplishments or attainments, rather than simply looking within the classroom at academic achievement, one finds the student's general intelligence status singularly unrevealing as to who is more likely to exhibit the superior performances. Instead, the clues are provided by information about the ideational resourcefulness of the person — something quite different from intelligence. As a result of these findings, we are led to the conclusion that decisions about the relative worthiness of students within the intelligence range that we have studied should rest heavily upon direct evidences of such forms of talented nonacademic accomplishments as we have examined. If, in other words, one is interested in future statesmen, one should select in terms of past evidences of social leadership; if one is interested in future writers, one should select in terms of past evidences of writing attainments; if one is interested in future scientists, one should select in terms of past evidences of scientific work;

and so on. In addition, our findings suggest that these decisions about relative worthiness also should rest upon indications of the person's characteristic level of ideational productivity — his readiness to generate ideational possibilities — as an index of his overall disposition toward innovating. The only warrant for making such decisions in terms of relative standing on intelligence would arise if one really wanted to sift off for preferential treatment, from among those students who already are expected to turn in quite creditable performances in the classroom, the ones who can be expected to earn still higher grades yet. But why would one ever, in fact, want to use academic achievement in this manner as an ultimate criterion? Its true value depends only, of course, on what it signifies. If we know that what we want to nourish is scientific talent, say, we clearly are better advised to select in terms of what seems to come closest to that criterion itself — signs of past attainments at science-related activities — and in terms of the generic cognitive disposition that seems to contribute to such accomplishments — namely, high ideational productivity. Intelligence level, after all, was related neither to our index of science-related accomplishments nor to the cognitive disposition in question.

It follows from the present discussion that what the educational establishment defines as "extracurricular" pursuits may well be worthy of more respectful treatment than such pursuits have tended to receive in the past. They provide us with indications of what the student is up to in those parts of his life where he is relatively on his own — where society permits him greater freedom to function autonomously. To that extent these pursuits have considerably more of a real-life flavor about them than the relatively artificial sequence of examinations and grades which schooling imposes upon him. Part of the psychological importance of nonacademic forms of talented accomplishments, then, is that they tell us something about what the student does because he wants to, rather than because of institutional pressures (see Frieden-berg, 1965; Nordstrom, Friedenberg, and Gold, 1967).

One could say, as a matter of fact, that our orientation in the present work has been toward delineating those students who most clearly are running on their own power in the world — the students who are most strongly committed to particular lines of endeavor which are carried on for reasons intrinsic to the tasks themselves. Recall in this connection our noting in the previous chapter that a sense of genuine commitment and the steering of a self-directed course maximally free from determination by societal expectations were most clearly in evidence for the students of high ideational productivity. We may be describing here the students whose internal resources provide the healthiest antidote against the pervasive forces abroad in the land that make for a sense of alienation and meaninglessness in so much of modern life — forces discussed in such recent social commentaries as, for instance, that provided by Keniston (1965). Perhaps the generating of ideational possibilities offers a key to the process whereby an individual comes to construct meaning for himself: he tries out ways of construing the environment that reflect his competencies and his sense of what is fitting, rather than passively digesting his culture's definition of what existence is all about.

How does one obtain, for purposes of making selections among students, information about talented nonacademic accomplishments and about level of ideational output? Perhaps one can adopt for selection purposes the approaches used in the research that we have described. On the other hand, these approaches may not prove to be applicable in practical selection contexts, because in such situations contingencies of great importance to the student hang upon how he responds. Thus, for example, veridicality of reports on nonacademic attainments might be impaired if winning a fellowship for a post-graduate year abroad depended upon what one said. So also, number of ideas offered as suggestions for how a shoe can be used would likely be inflated if the student suspected that giving a larger number of ideas made admission to graduate school more probable. When the student knows that selection for preferential treatment depends on how he responds, therefore, more subtle ways of obtaining information about nonacademic accomplishments and about ideational resourcefulness may be in order. One could, for instance, seek to assess nonacademic attainments through direct evidence that a poetry prize was won, a short story was published, or a painting was exhibited. And one might seek to assess ideational resourcefulness through training interviewers in the art of probing the extent of the spontaneous nonacademic thoughts of the interviewee.

The contribution of the present investigation, then, has not been to solve the practical selection problem, but rather to obtain the research findings that indicate a practical selection problem exists. In the light of our evidence, it is clear that a wide range of talented accomplishments that the society wants to sustain and nourish are lost to view when one relies too heavily upon intelligence assessment for selection purposes; and furthermore, that many of these accomplishments are supported by a kind of ideational ability which itself is quite extraneous to the intelligence concept as well. The present findings hence provide a demonstration that alternative bases for talent identification are essential, and a set of substantive guidelines as to what sorts of alternatives are needed.

Besides the matter of proceeding to the arena of application, there are other tasks too which the present work leaves as unfinished business for the future. Recall that what we have demonstrated refers to a student sample that can be characterized as having SAT scores falling within the upper half of the overall score distribution for those high school seniors who take the SAT. The generalizations that follow directly from our findings thus pertain to the upper ranges of the intelligence continuum. Just how far down one could move along the intelligence dimension and still find the present generalizations holding remains an open question that can only be decided by further research. It is worth entertaining very seriously the possibility, however, that what we have found to hold across the upper reaches of the intelligence spread may hold for the middle parts of the scale as well.

Another step in need of pursuit is the carrying out of a long-term follow-up that traces students of the types here defined as they proceed to navigate life's course when the undergraduate years are over. Who turn out in fact to become the political leaders, the artists, the writers, the scientists, the actors, the musicians — and to excel in their contributions to such fields? What we have argued for represents a different way of placing one's bets in these matters; a way which our findings suggest will yield greater fruit than would be obtained by depending on intelligence assessment.

Viewed in its most general perspective, the work reported here makes the following quite plain. If comprehension and nourishment of the full spectrum of talents displayed by students is our goal, we must look elsewhere for enlightenment than just toward the intelligence concept. One psychological realm toward which we clearly should look in this regard concerns the characteristic degrees of resourcefulness exhibited by the students in generating ideas — what we have come to call their level of cognitive vitality or energy.

References

BARRON, F. The disposition toward originality. *Journal of Abnormal and Social Psychology*, 1955, **51**, 478–485.

BARRON, F. Originality in relation to personality and intellect. *Journal of Personality*, 1957, **25**, 730–742.

BARRON, F. *Creativity and psychological health*. Princeton, N. J.: Van Nostrand, 1963.

BEREITER, C. Fluency abilities in preschool children. *Journal of Genetic Psychology*, 1961, **98**, 47–48.

BOERSMA, F. J., & O'BRYAN, K. An investigation of the relationship between creativity and intelligence under two conditions of testing. *Journal of Personality*, 1968, *36*, 341–348.

BONEAU, C. A. The effects of violations of assumptions underlying the *t* test. *Psychological Bulletin*, 1960, **57**, 49–64.

BRUNSWIK, E. *Perception and the representative design of psychological experiments*. Berkeley: University of California Press, 1956.

CHRISTENSEN, P. R., GUILFORD, J. P., & WILSON, R. C. Relations of creative responses to working time and instructions. *Journal of Experimental Psychology*, 1957, **53**, 82–88.

CLARK, C. M., VELDMAN, D. J., & THORPE, J. S. Convergent and divergent thinking abilities of talented adolescents. *Journal of Educational Psychology*, 1965, **56**, 157–163.

COLLEGE ENTRANCE EXAMINATION BOARD. *Validity study service: Data analysis and interpretation.* New York: 1964.

COLLEGE ENTRANCE EXAMINATION BOARD. *College Board score reports: A guide for counselors and admissions officers.* New York: 1966.

DAVIDSEN, O. M. Reliability of self-reported high school grades. Unpublished research report, American College Testing Program, Iowa City, Iowa, 1963.

EDWARDS, M. P., & TYLER, LEONA E. Intelligence, creativity, and achievement in a nonselective public junior high school. *Journal of Educational Psychology*, 1965, **56,** 96–99.

FELDHUSEN, J. F., DENNY, T., & CONDON, C. F. Anxiety, divergent thinking, and achievement. *Journal of Educational Psychology*, 1965, **56,** 40–45.

FRIEDENBERG, E. Z. *Coming of age in America: Growth and acquiescence.* New York: Random House, 1965.

GARWOOD, DOROTHY S. Personality factors related to creativity in young scientists. *Journal of Abnormal and Social Psychology*, 1964, **68,** 413–419.

GEWIRTZ, J. L. Studies in word fluency. I. Its relation to vocabulary and mental age in young children. *Journal of Genetic Psychology*, 1948, **72,** 165–176. (a)

GEWIRTZ, J. L. Studies in word fluency. II. Its relation to eleven items of child behavior. *Journal of Genetic Psychology*, 1948, **72,** 177–184. (b)

GHISELIN, B. (Ed.) *The creative process.* New York: Mentor, 1955.

GUILFORD, J. P. Three faces of intellect. *American Psychologist*, 1959, **14,** 469–479.

GUILFORD, J. P. Some new looks at the nature of creative processes. In N. Frederiksen and H. Gulliksen (Eds.), *Contributions to mathematical psychology.* New York: Holt, Rinehart and Winston, 1964. Pp. 161–176.

GUILFORD, J. P. *The nature of human intelligence.* New York: McGraw-Hill, 1967.

HOLLAND, J. L. Creative and academic performance among talented adolescents. *Journal of Educational Psychology*, 1961, **52,** 136–147.

HOLLAND, J. L. The prediction of academic and nonacademic accomplishment. In *Proceedings of the 1966 invitational conference on testing problems.* Princeton, N. J.: Educational Testing Service, 1967. Pp. 44–51.

HOLLAND, J. L., & NICHOLS, R. C. Prediction of academic and extra-curricular achievement in college. *Journal of Educational Psychology*, 1964, **55**, 55–65.

HOLLAND, J. L., & RICHARDS, J. M., JR. Academic and nonacademic accomplishment: Correlated or uncorrelated? *Journal of Educational Psychology*, 1965, **56**, 165–174.

HOLLAND, J. L., & RICHARDS, J. M., JR. Academic and nonacademic achievement in a representative sample taken from a population of 612,000. Unpublished research report, American College Testing Program, Iowa City, Iowa, 1966.

HOLLAND, J. L., & RICHARDS, J. M., JR. The many faces of talent: A reply to Werts. *Journal of Educational Psychology*, 1967, **58**, 205–209.

HOYT, D. P. College grades and adult accomplishment: A review of research. *The Educational Record*, 1966 (Winter), 70–75.

KENISTON, K. *The uncommitted: Alienated youth in American society.* New York: Harcourt, Brace and World, 1965.

KOGAN, N., & MORGAN, F. T. Task and motivational influences on the assessment of creative and intellective ability in children. Unpublished research report, Educational Testing Service, Princeton, N. J., 1967.

MAY, F. B., & METCALF, A. W. A factor-analytic study of spontaneous-flexibility measures. *Educational and Psychological Measurement*, 1965, **25**, 1039–1050.

McGUIRE, C., HINDSMAN, E., KING, F. J., & JENNINGS, E. Dimensions of talented behavior. *Educational and Psychological Measurement*, 1961, **21**, 3–38.

NORDSTROM, C., FRIEDENBERG, E. Z., & GOLD, H. A. *Society's children: A study of ressentiment in the secondary school.* New York: Random House, 1967.

ORPET, R. E., & MEYERS, C. E. Six structure-of-intellect hypotheses in six-year-old children. *Journal of Educational Psychology*, 1966, **57**, 341–346.

RICHARDS, J. M., JR., HOLLAND, J. L., & LUTZ, SANDRA W. The assessment of student accomplishment in college. Unpublished research report, American College Testing Program, Iowa City, Iowa, 1966.

RICHARDS, J. M., JR., HOLLAND, J. L., & LUTZ, SANDRA W. Prediction of student accomplishment in college. *Journal of Educational Psychology*, 1967, **58**, 343–355.

THORNDIKE, R. L. The measurement of creativity. *Teachers College Record*, 1963, **64**, 422–424. (a)

THORNDIKE, R. L. Some methodological issues in the study of creativity. In *Proceedings of the 1962 invitational conference on testing problems.* Princeton, N. J.: Educational Testing Service, 1963. Pp. 40–54. (b)

WALLACH, M. A. Creativity and the expression of possibilities. In J. Kagan (Ed.), *Creativity and learning.* Boston: Houghton Mifflin, 1967. Pp. 36–57.

WALLACH, M. A. Creativity. In P. H. Mussen (Ed.), *Manual of child psychology.* New York: Wiley, in press.

WALLACH, M. A., & KOGAN, N. *Modes of thinking in young children: A study of the creativity-intelligence distinction.* New York: Holt, Rinehart and Winston, 1965.

WARD, W. C. Creativity in young children. *Child Development,* 1968, *39,* 737–754.

WECHSLER, D. *The measurement of adult intelligence,* Ed. 3. Baltimore: Williams and Wilkins, 1952.

WERTS, C. E. The many faces of intelligence. *Journal of Educational Psychology,* 1967, **58,** 198–204.

Name Index

Barron, F., 18
Bereiter, C., 17
Boersma, F. J., 16
Boneau, C. A., 51
Brunswik, E., 3

Cage, J., 21
Christensen, P. R., 15
Clark, C. M., 17
Condon, C. F., 18

Davidsen, O. M., 7
Denny, T., 18
Dryden, J., 20, 21

Edwards, M. P., 2

Feldhusen, J. F., 18
Friedenberg, E. Z., 129

Garwood, Dorothy S., 18, 19
Gewirtz, J. L., 17
Ghiselin, B., 20
Gold, H. A., 129
Guilford, J. P., 13, 15

Hindsman, E., 17

Subject Index

Academic achievement, in college, 60–63
  in high school, 54–60
  and ideational productivity, 54–63
  and ideational uniqueness, 54–63
  and intelligence, 54–63
  theoretical issues concerning, 1–25
Achievement motivation, 9–10
Agreement in judging uniqueness, 36–37
Art attainments, procedure for assessing, 66
  results and interpretation for, 82–85
  see also Talented nonacademic accomplishments

Class rank, 54–60
Classroom achievement, *see* Academic achievement
Cognitive energy level, 16, 20, 22, 58, 78, 84, 91, 94, 99, 108–110, 125–131
  see also Ideational productivity
Cognitive vitality, *see* Cognitive energy level
College academic achievement, 60–63
College Entrance Examination Board, 28–29, 55–56
Creativity, theoretical issues concerning, 12–25
  see also Ideational productivity
  see also Ideational uniqueness

139

Intelligence, and academic achievement, 54–63
and ideational productivity, 26–53
and ideational uniqueness, 26–53
implications of results concerning, 124–131
and talented nonacademic accomplishments, 64–110
theoretical issues concerning, 1–25
Internal consistency of each ideational task, 39–41
Interviews, 111–123
conclusions from, 121–123
Intrinsic motivation, 122, 128–129

Leadership attainments, procedure for assessing, 66
results and interpretation for, 79–82
see also Talented nonacademic accomplishments
Line-meanings task, instructions for, 33–34
Literary attainments, procedure for assessing, 66–67
results and interpretation for, 88–91
see also Talented nonacademic accomplishments
Logics, non-Aristotelian, 20

Manual, for scoring idea differences, 34–36

Miller Analogies Test, 124, 126
see also Intelligence
Motivation, for achievement, 9–10
intrinsic, 122, 128–129
for novelty, 16, 20, 22–23, 110
Musical attainments, procedure for assessing, 67
results and interpretation for, 95–98
see also Talented nonacademic accomplishments

Nonacademic accomplishments, *see* Talented nonacademic accomplishments
Number of ideas, *see* Ideational productivity

Output of ideas, *see* Ideational productivity

Pattern-meanings task, instructions for, 32–33
Performance and production skills compared, 93–98
Production and performance skills compared, 93–98
Productivity of ideas, *see* Ideational productivity

Quality point ratio, 60–63